THE INTERNET ANSWER BOOK

For Human Resource Professionals

Mark M. Moran
Alexander M. Padro

MORAN ASSOCIATES
Orange Park, FL

Moran Associates, 1600 Brighton Bluff Court, Orange Park, FL 32073 • Phone: 904-278-5155 Toll Free: 1-800-597-2040 • Fax: 904-278-5494 E-mail: smoran@webtv.net

Copyright © 1997 Moran Associates

All rights reserved. No part of this publication may be reproduced, stored in a retrieval system, or transmitted in any form or by any means, electronic, mechanical, photocopying, recording, or otherwise, without the prior written permission of the copyright owners.

Every effort has been made to supply complete and accurate information. However, neither the publisher nor the authors assume any responsibility for its use, nor for any infringement of the intellectual property rights of third parties which could result from such use.

Photographs and illustrations used in this book have been downloaded from publicly accessible file archives and are used in this book for news reportage purposes only to demonstrate the variety of graphics resources available via electronic access. The source of each photograph or illustration is identified. Text and images available over the Internet may be subject to copyright and other rights owned by third parties. Online availability of text and images does not imply that they may be reused without the permission of rights holders, although the Copyright Act does permit certain unauthorized reuse as fair use under 17 U.S.C. § 107. Care should be taken to ensure that all necessary rights are cleared prior to reusing material distributed over the Internet. Information about reuse rights is available from the institutions who make their material available over the Internet.

First Edition   ISBN 1-890966-00-2

Printed in the United States of America

00 99 98 97   5 4 3 2 1

CONTENTS

DEDICATION — xi
ACKNOWLEDGMENTS — xiii
ABOUT THE AUTHORS — xiv
INTRODUCTION — xv

CHAPTER 1
WHAT IS THE INTERNET? 1

A NETWORK OF COMPUTERS — 3
    History of the Internet — 4
    An Information Superhighway — 6
WHAT DO I NEED TO GO ONLINE? — 6
WHO IS USING THE INTERNET? — 6

CHAPTER 2
ANSWERS TO FREQUENTLY ASKED QUESTIONS ABOUT THE INTERNET 9

WHAT IS A FAQ? — 11
WHAT IS THE INTERNET? — 12
    Who Runs the Internet? — 12
    How Big is the Internet? — 13

HOW DO I CONNECT TO THE INTERNET? 14

How is the Internet Different from Commercial
    Online Services? 14
What Internet Tools Do Commercial Online
    Services Offer? 15
What's the Difference Between an ISP and an
    Online Service? 15

WHO'S THE BEST INTERNET PROVIDER? 16

WHAT KIND OF INFORMATION IS AVAILABLE
ON THE INTERNET? 17

WHO PUTS INFORMATION ON THE
INTERNET? 17

WHY SHOULD I USE THE INTERNET? 17

HOW DO I FIND HUMAN RESOURCES
INFORMATION ON THE WORLD
WIDE WEB? 20

    How Do I Search Human Resource
        Newsgroups? 21
    What is FTP? 21
    What is Archie? 21
    What About Gopher and Veronica? 22

WHAT DOES URL MEAN? 22

WHAT IS A MAILING LIST? 24

HOW DO I SEND ELECTRONIC MAIL TO
HR PROFESSIONALS ON ONLINE
SERVICES? 24

HOW CAN I USE THE INTERNET TO TALK
WITH OTHER HUMAN RESOURCES
PROFESSIONALS? 25

CHAPTER 3
HOW DO I GET STARTED? 27

WHAT DO I NEED? 29

Table of Contents v

EQUIPMENT REQUIREMENTS	29
Memory	29
Modems	30
TELEPHONE LINES	31
ISDN	31
INTERNET ACCESS	32
ONLINE SERVICES VERSUS INTERNET SERVICE PROVIDERS	32
ONLINE SERVICES	33
America Online	33
CompuServe	34
The Microsoft Network	36
Prodigy	37
Which Service is Right for You?	38
INTERNET SERVICE PROVIDERS	39
Basics	40
Connections	40
Pricing	41
Going It Alone	41
On-line Advice on Choosing An ISP	42
Other Resources for Choosing a Provider	42
PHONE COMPANIES GET INTO THE ACT	44
Internet MCI	44
AT&T World Net Services	44
OTHER SELECTION CONSIDERATIONS	44
Protocols	44
SLIP and CSLIP	45
PPP	45
Which is better: SLIP or PPP?	45
SLIP/PPP Services	45
WEB BROWSERS	46

To Buy or Not to Buy?	46
Netscape Navigator	47
Microsoft Internet Explorer	48

CHAPTER 4
WHAT IS ELECTRONIC MAIL? 51

THE MOST POPULAR ONLINE TOOL	53
E-MAIL SOFTWARE	56
E-MAIL IS NO LAUGHING MATTER	59

CHAPTER 5
WHAT ARE NEWSGROUPS AND MAILING LISTS? 63

WHAT ARE NEWSGROUPS?	65
HOW IS USENET ORGANIZED?	66
The Seven Standard USENET Group Categories	66
Alternative Newsgroups	67
SELECTING NEWSREADER SOFTWARE	68
Newsreader Software Options	68
Netscape	68
Microsoft Internet News	68
How do I Search Human Resource Newsgroups?	69
WHAT IS A MAILING LIST?	69
Moderated Mailing Lists	70
Digests	70
Finding Lists	70
HOW TO SUBSCRIBE TO A MAILING LIST	71
Subscribe	71
Unsubscribe	72
MAILING LIST ETIQUETTE	72

HOW CAN I CHAT ONLINE?	72
What is IRC?	72

CHAPTER 6
A DIRECTORY OF HUMAN RESOURCES NEWSGROUPS AND MAILING LISTS 75

HUMAN RESOURCES NEWSGROUPS	77
HUMAN RESOURCES MAILING LISTS	79

CHAPTER 7
WHAT ABOUT THE WORLD WIDE WEB? 85

"WHAT CAN THE WEB DO FOR ME?"	87
WHAT IS THE WORLD WIDE WEB (WWW)?	88
Hyperlinks	88
HOW DOES THE WEB WORK?	89
World Wide Web Addresses	89
What is a Web Page?	90
Should You Have a Web Site?	91

CHAPTER 8
HOW CAN I GET WHAT I WANT FROM THE INTERNET? 93

NET TOOLS	95
TELNET	95
GOPHER	96
How does Gopher differ from the Web?	96
How does Gopher work?	96
Advanced functions	98
VERONICA	98
ARCHIE	99

WAIS	100
FTP	101
WHAT IS A SEARCH ENGINE?	102
CHOOSING A SEARCH ENGINE	103
Alta Vista	103
Excite	104
Info Seek	105
Lycos	106
Web Crawler	107
Yahoo	108

CHAPTER 9
A DIRECTORY OF HUMAN RESOURCES WEB SITES............ 111

ADDICTION	113
AFFIRMATIVE ACTION	114
ASSESSMENT	116
ASSOCIATIONS	116
BEHAVIOR AT WORK	122
BENEFITS	123
BUSINESS INFORMATION	131
COMPENSATION	132
COUNSELING SERVICES	135
DEVELOPMENT	135
DISABILITY	137
DIVERSITY	139
EMPLOYEE OWNERSHIP	140
EMPLOYEE RELATIONS	140
EMPLOYMENT DISCRIMINATION	143
ERGONOMICS	145

GENERAL	146
HEALTH PROMOTION	147
INTRANETS	150
JOB SEARCH SKILLS	151
LABOR-MANAGEMENT RELATIONS	157
LAWS AND REGULATIONS	159
MANAGEMENT CONSULTANTS	163
MEDIATION AND DISPUTE RESOLUTION	165
OTHER RESOURCES	167
OUTPLACEMENT	170
PAYROLL	171
QUALITY	172
RECRUITMENT	173
RELOCATION	179
SAFETY	180
SECURITY	184
SELECTION	185
SEXUAL HARRASSMENT	187
SMOKING	188
SOFTWARE/TECHNOLOGY	188
STATISTICS	198
TAXES	200
TELECOMMUTING	201
TEMPORARY AND ALTERNATIVE STAFFING	202
TRAINING	204
WEB INDEXES	211

WOMEN'S ISSUES	215
WORKPLACE VIOLENCE	216

CHAPTER 10
WHAT ABOUT...? 219

AN ADDRESS LISTED IN THIS BOOK DOESN'T WORK. WHY NOT?	221
E-mail	221
World Wide Web and Gopher	222
Newsgroups	223
WHAT IS LEGAL TO PUT ON THE INTERNET?	223
ARE THERE RULES ON HOW TO COMMUNICATE ON THE INTERNET?	224
SHOULD I WORRY ABOUT THE PRIVACY OF MY INTERNET TRANSMISSIONS?	225
How Can I Ensure the Privacy of What I Send Via the Internet?	226
Is It Safe to Send My Credit Card Number Over the Internet?	227
WHAT DO I NEED TO KNOW ABOUT COMPUTER VIRUSES?	227
HOW CAN A HUMAN RESOURCES PROFESSIONAL CREATE A WEB PAGE?	228
IS THERE A LOT OF PORNOGRAPHY ON THE INTERNET?	229

CHAPTER 11
WHAT DOES THAT MEAN? 231

INDEX 241

DEDICATION

To today's human resource professionals, who continue to hire, train, and develop the world's workforce despite constantly increasing challenges.

ACKNOWLEDGMENTS

The authors would like to thank Cleone Brock and Pam Hanks for their assistance in the preparation of the manuscript for this book, and Richard Austin for the cover design concept.

Special thanks go to Pleasant P. Mann, without whose technical knowledge of the Internet and desktop publishing skills, this book would have been far less authoritative and much less attractive.

ABOUT THE AUTHORS

Mark M. Moran is president of Moran Associates, a management consulting firm offering human resource professionals a variety of services, including OSHA compliance assistance. He is the author of over two dozen books and electronic products, including the best-selling *OSHA Answer Book*.

Alexander M. Padro is a book publishing professional with over 10 years experience in acquisitions, development, production, and marketing of books on business, education, law, science, and engineering. A member of the Washington Book Publishers, he holds a degree in journalism from New York University.

INTRODUCTION

The Internet has become as indispensable to human resource professionals as computers, fax machines, and telephone service. But even though many HR professionals currently use the Net regularly, countless others are still unfamiliar with the Internet, the World Wide Web, and the vast HR resources available online.

The purpose of this book is to provide you, the human resource professional, with an understanding of what the Net has to offer and how to use this exciting resource to assist you in planning and making decisions.

In addtion to explaining how the Internet works, what software, hardware, and services you need to get online, and the basics of e-mail, mailing lists, discussion groups, and Web sites, three directories provide descriptions of over 600 of the best Internet resources on 44 HR topics. This is the most extensive reference available covering Internet resources for the HR community, saving the reader countless hours and considerable online or service provider fees.

It is impossible to truly grasp the immense resources the Internet offers by reading a newspaper or magazine article or even this book. But we hope *The Internet Answer Book for Human Resource Professionals* will inspire and help you to discover for yourself the benefits and competitive advantages of being online.

We welcome you comments on this book, as well as your suggestions for additions to the directory chapters. You can contact us via e-mail at **smoran@webtv.net** or

ampadro@aol.com, or via snail mail at MORAN ASSOCIATES, 1600 Brighton Bluff Court, Orange Park, FL 32073.

Mark M. Moran
Alexander M. Padro

CHAPTER 1

WHAT IS THE INTERNET?

CHAPTER 1

WHAT IS THE INTERNET?

A NETWORK OF COMPUTERS

There are many definitions of what the Internet is. The easiest way to view the Internet is as a large network of computers (in reality, it's the world's largest), like the typical office network illustrated below.

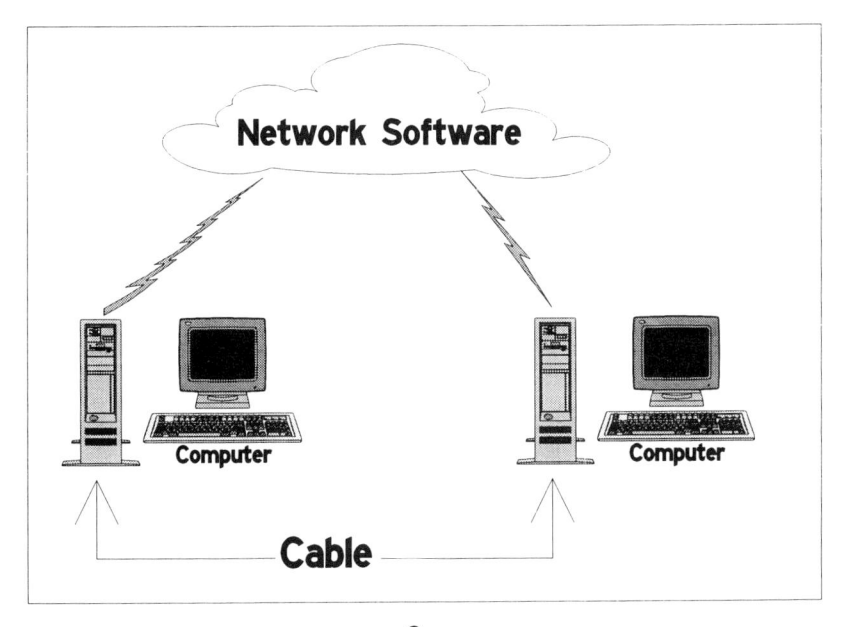

The Internet is simply a larger version of the system shown in the earlier illustration. But instead of two computers sharing information, there are up to 50 million computers sharing

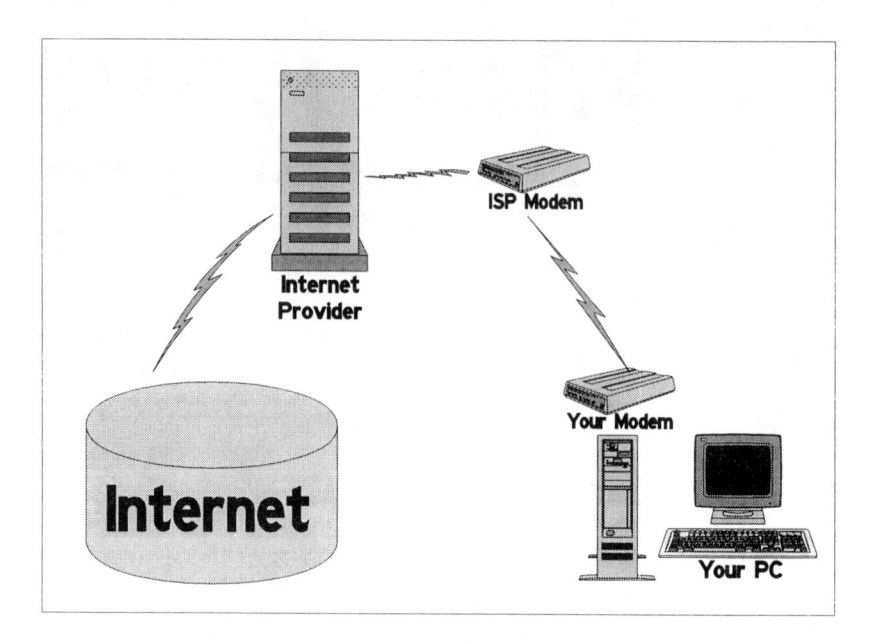

information. We use cables and software to share information across the network. The cables are the telephone lines that connect you to your service provider. The software allows you to access your provider and the Internet.

Once you have connected to the Internet, you have a wide range of activities you can engage in. You can send e-mail. You can search over 21 million Web pages on the World Wide Web for human resources information. You can ask thousands of human resources colleagues how they solved problems your company faces. You can find all kinds of information on human resources online.

For the first time ever, the world is truly at your fingertips.

History of the Internet

One of the curious things about the Internet is that it was never designed to be large—quite the opposite, in fact. Just like how our federal government began some two hundred years ago.

What Is the Internet?

Ironically, today's popular Internet is a relic of the secretive atmosphere of the Cold War. The roots of the Internet were created by, you guessed it, the U.S. Armed Forces.

The Advanced Research Projects Agency Network (ARPANET) was created by the U.S. Department of Defense in the late 1960's. It was designed to be a defense-oriented nationwide computer network capable, among other things, of withstanding a nuclear attack.

The integrity of the ARPA network was ensured by building in redundancy. Data traveling from one computer to another could take any one of many routes to its destination. If part of the network was destroyed by a nuclear attack, it would automatically route data via an alternate path.

ARPANET was also designed to break the data stream transmitted over the network into small packets of information, like dividing a long letter into hundreds of individual postcards, so that if one postcard failed to arrive at its destination, it could easily be sent again. Called Transmission Control Protocol/Internet Protocol (TCP/IP), this is the language spoken by every computer on the Internet today. This common language allows all sorts of computers—from PCs and Macintoshes to mainframes and supercomputers—to exchange data over the Internet.

When the likelihood of nuclear attack decreased, the network was gradually demilitarized, becoming a largely academic enterprise tying together researchers and students at colleges, corporations, and research institutions around the world.

The Internet grew gradually over the 1970's and 1980's, but access was mostly restricted to academia. But with the personal computer boom, commercial Internet service providers began making it possible for the general public to access the Net. While home computer ownership in the 1980's led to the enormous growth of online services (such as pioneers CompuServe and Prodigy), as well as thousands of local computer bulletin boards, these services remained completely separate from the Internet until 1993. As the gates to the Internet finally started opening up, what had begun as a slow trickle of interest turned into today's tidal wave of new Internet users.

An Information Superhighway

The term information superhighway is perhaps an unfortunate one, but it is meaningful for U.S. Vice President Al Gore, whose father championed the interstate superhighway system. Following in his father's footsteps, Gore has been pushing for federal support for the information superhighway. The Clinton administration's plans for the information superhighway's development call for cooperation between the private and public sectors in building the system. The private sector would construct and operate the backbone networks and delivery systems, while the public sector would pass laws encouraging private investment in the system.

While publicity about the information superhighway gives the impression that most American homes already have some type of computer access, the truth is that only 32 percent of households have computers. And only half of those machines have modems that can connect computers with each other via telephone lines.

While it will likely be some time before every household in America has Internet access, most businesses, colleges and universities can currently access the Net. And a wide variety of companies, professional organizations, and government agencies have Web sites in place which allow users to obtain information of value to human resources managers.

WHAT DO I NEED TO GO ONLINE?

The computer on your desk is probaly powerful enough to access the Internet. In addition, you will need a modem, a phone line, and an account with an Internet Service Provider (ISP). More information on hardware and software requirements is provided in Chapter 3.

WHO IS USING THE INTERNET?

The answer is millions of people worldwide. The number and diversity of people using the Internet is growing at an

What Is the Internet?

amazing rate, with the most explosive growth occurring on the World Wide Web. While there are millions of parents and children using the Web, online services, and newsgroups for entertainment, there are also countless professionals in every field of endeavor sharing and seeking information in their areas of expertise.

Both government and businesses have recognized that the Internet is a vast and inexpensive way to distribute information to a large number of people. Product manufacturers, service providers, government agencies and officials, newspapers and magazines, and others are providing significant online resources of use to the human resources profession.

For example, a very useful site for HR professionals is provided by the U.S. Department of Labor's Occupational Safety and Health Administration. This site includes detailed information on safety and health regulations your company must

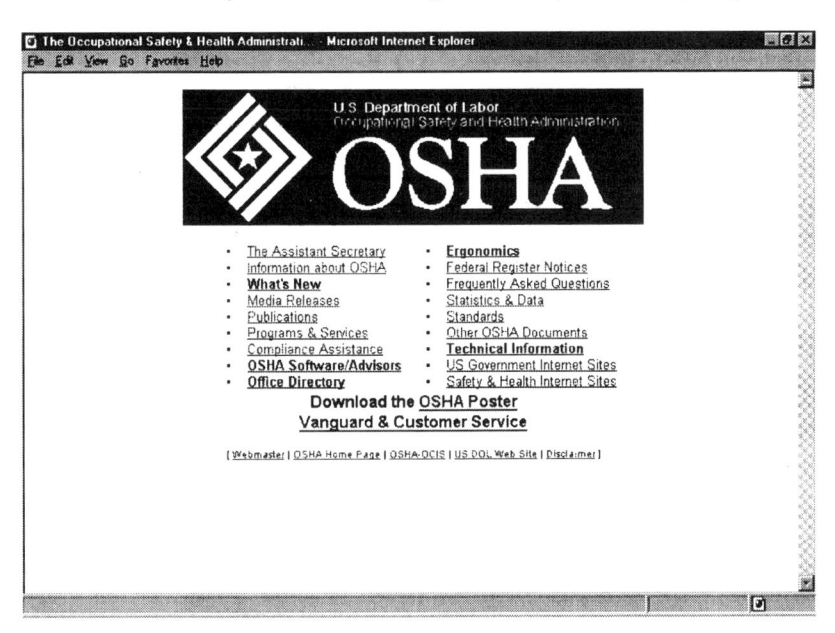

comply with. It includes news releases of interest to the many HR managers who are responsible for workplace safety issues.

Another useful site is provided by the G. Neil Company, suppliers of a wide variety of products for human resource management. If you need a particular poster, form or award, you can find out if it is available and how to order it, even on weekends.

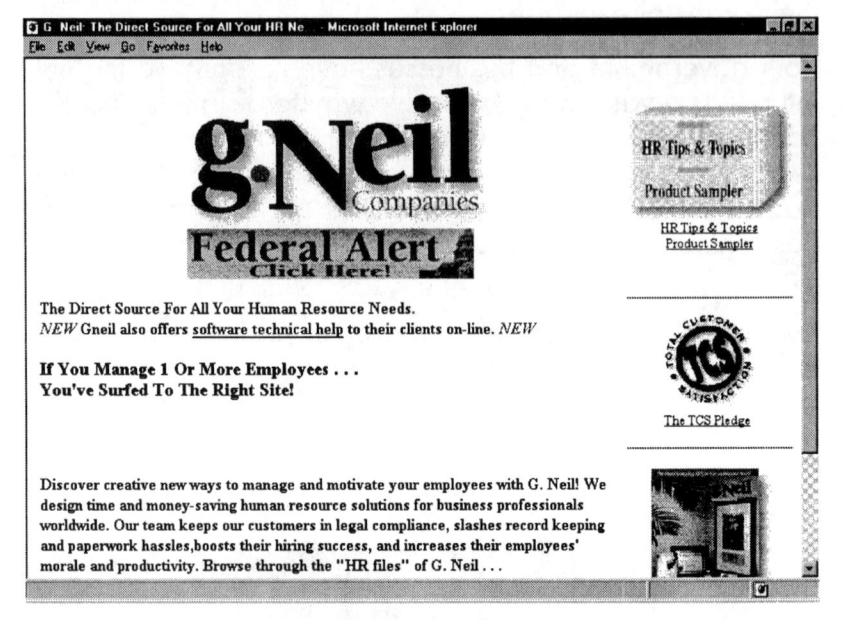

The Internet is truly a tool for everyone to use, from human resource professionals to CEOs. No matter who you are, or what you are interested in, there is a place for you on the Web. Ultimately, the answer to who uses the Web is *you*!

CHAPTER 2
ANSWERS TO FREQUENTLY ASKED QUESTIONS ABOUT THE INTERNET

CHAPTER 2
ANSWERS TO FREQUENTLY ASKED QUESTIONS ABOUT THE INTERNET

WHAT IS A FAQ?

A FAQ is a file with Frequently Asked Questions and their answers, which are provided by many newsgroups so that new users can have their questions answered without repeatedly subjecting all participants to those questions. To answer both basic and advanced questions, we have prepared a FAQ which summarizes most of the questions readers are likely to have about the Internet.

Some of these questions cover the nuts-and-bolts details of using Internet tools. Others are about making the best possible use of Internet resources, understanding how newsgroups work, or how to behave in certain areas of the Internet.

Many of these questions are dealt with in the following chapters. However, you may find this FAQ a helpful overview of what the Internet has to offer before you embark on your first online experience.

WHAT IS THE INTERNET?

The Internet began as an experiment more than 25 years ago by the U.S. Department of Defense. This agency created a network called ARPANET, to support military research. It was linked to other networks around the world. ARPANET grew beyond the wildest expectations of its creators. The massive hodgepodge of interconnected networks became known as the Internet. Today, the Internet is the world's largest computer network, spanning nearly the entire globe and meeting the needs of an estimated 35 million people worldwide.

You may be familiar with commercial online services such as The Microsoft Network, American Online, CompuServe, and Prodigy. All of these services are part of the Internet (they each provide their users access to certain Internet resources), but the services themselves are only a small part of the whole.

Other pieces of the Internet puzzle include Internet Service Providers (ISPs), companies that provide individuals and businesses with access to the Internet network, and businesses and organizations, both public and private, that have their own Internet access. These millions of individual components make up the Internet.

Who Runs the Internet?

For the most part, the Internet community runs itself In this case, however, anarchy does not mean "every man for himself." Instead, every organization and individual that is connected to the Internet is responsible for its own part.

A remarkable characteristic of this arrangement is that members of the Internet community are known for their willingness to assist others. In USENET newsgroups, users frequently advise and answer the questions of total strangers. Businesses connected to the Internet frequently exchange technical help and services on an informal basis. And countless individuals and organizations put in long hours posting free information online.

But there are rules on the Internet, and they are collectively called "netiquette." The Internet is "self-policing," so there are no "Net cops" to pull you over to the side of the information superhighway and write you a ticket. On the other hand, if you break a rule, you'll probably receive a few (or even a few dozen) messages from fellow Internet users, showing you the error of your ways.

In terms of charting a course for the future of the Net, ultimate authority rests with the Internet Society (ISOC). ISOC is a voluntary membership organization whose purpose if to promote global information exchange through Internet technology. It appoints a council (called the Internet Architecture Board, or IAB), which has responsibility for the technical management and direction of the Internet.

How Big is the Internet?

According to some estimates, there are approximately 35 million people with Internet access worldwide. But some believe this number is too high or too low, but because of the decentralized nature of the Internet, it is very difficult to monitor its size or rate of growth.

You can measure parts of the Internet, such as the number of servers in a given area, but it's harder to pinpoint the exact number of people with access to the Net. In the words of Internet expert John S. Quarterman, "Because no single entity is in control, nobody knows everything about the Internet. Measuring it is especially hard because some parts choose to limit access to themselves to various degrees. So, instead of measurement, we have various forms of surveying and estimation."

However, what is certain is that the Internet is growing very quickly and probably will continue its exponential growth for some time to come.

HOW DO I CONNECT TO THE INTERNET?

Relatively few computers are directly connected to the fastest part of the Internet, called the "backbone." These backbone systems are most often found at universities, research institutions, and government agencies, or are Baby Bells and long distance services that own their own cables.

Most people and companies have to connect to the Internet through a commercial Internet Service Provider (ISP). An ISP is a subscription service, much like cable TV. There are the big four commercial online services (America Online, Prodigy, CompuServe, and Microsoft Network). You will pay a monthly fee and the ISP provides you with access to the Internet backbone.

It works a lot like a toll booth for a bridge or tunnel. You have to pay a fee before you can drive across the bridge or though the tunnel. An ISP, then, is the "toll booth" where you stop and pay before you can access the information superhighway. In fact, an ISP is often called an Internet "gateway" because it's the gate your computer connection has to pass through in order to get onto the Internet backbone.

How is the Internet Different from Commercial Online Services?

The Internet and commercial online services are related (in some ways they are even becoming intertwined), but they aren't the same thing. For instance, consider how you connect to the Internet. You can access the Internet by using an ISP, or by using a commercial online service such as America Online or Prodigy. ISPs provide an on-ramp to the Internet. Their function is to provide a gateway to information. They are not in the business of creating content themselves.

On the other hand, commercial online services usually provide their own content. You can use these services to do things that aren't necessarily available on the Internet, like search an encyclopedia, read today's news headlines, and get stock market information. Online services also serve as

ISPs, providing users access to the Internet. It is worth noting that online services' customized content is not available to Internet users who don't subscribe to that particular online service.

The boundary between what a commercial online service and the Internet can offer is rapidly disappearing. Until recently, you couldn't find reference material or today's sports scores on the Net. If you wanted that information online you needed to use on online service. Today, all of these services are available on the Internet, sometimes at a price, but often for free.

Online services do have advantages. Online services are generally much better organized than the Internet. A single directory can usually provide access to all features. But online services frequently have a less diverse set of opinions and attitudes than the Internet community at large.

What Internet Tools Do Commercial Online Services Offer?

Each service has its own features, but it is safe to say that all online services now offer nearly full access to Internet resources, including e-mail, newsgroups, and the World Wide Web. Differences between commercial online services are primarily in their user interfaces and pricing structures.

What's the Difference Between an ISP and an Online Service?

Many people don't understand the distinction. An ISP provides Internet access, and that's all. Once your computer passes through your ISP's gateway, you're on your own, free to explore the chaotic Internet, but also free to get lost on any of a number of information byways.

An online service (like CompuServe, American Online, Prodigy, or The Microsoft Network) organizes all it's features neatly into categories and menus and provide lots of online help to users. Companies that provide features and services (news, weather, etc.) pay a fee to do so, or pay a cut of their profits to the online service. The bottom line is that an online service exercises complete control over the vendors and organizations that reside online and controls which areas subscribers can visit and how much subscribers should be charged for browsing the service's different areas.

Your ISP determines how much to charge you for access to the Internet and how much time you can spend on the Internet. But beyond that, you're on your own, free to explore all of the far reaches of the Net. The Internet isn't very organized, because there's no single company or organization to control it, unlike the way online services operate.

Now here's where the line gets blurry. Most of the major online services have come to realize that the only way to compete with the Internet is to provide subscribers with access to the Internet. In this sense, an online service is also an ISP.

For instance, America Online provides some dialog boxes that allow you to connect to different parts of the Internet, but once you venture out on to the Internet itself, you're beyond the controlled scope of AOL. In other words, AOL provides an interface and a gateway for connecting to the Internet. But once you pass through this gateway, you're technically outside of AOL's control. You now run the potential of getting "lost in cyberspace," a risk that most new Internet travelers have to come to terms with.

WHO'S THE BEST INTERNET PROVIDER?

What do you mean by "best?" For many people, it means cheapest. Right now, what's cheap are shell accounts and freenets. For people who aren't computer-savvy, these accounts might be a difficult place to start.

What do you plan to do on the Internet? If all you want is e-mail and access to the World Wide Web, almost any account will do, but the price ranges vary widely, so how easy it is to get started may be the deciding factor for you. If you've never used a computer in your life and think that you might get easily frustrated, choose a commercial service that tries to make your experience easier.

If you're more patient and want to save money, you can try a SLIP/PPP or shell account. Depending on where you live, you might not have that much of a choice. If you do have a choice, find out how much help is available from your provider. Talking to service providers before you begin can give you valuable insight into which service is best for you.

WHAT KIND OF INFORMATION IS AVAILABLE ON THE INTERNET?

No matter what your interest, there is something for you on the Internet. Whether you are a human resource professional or a student seeking a job in computer programming, you will find something relating to your interests on the Net. There are millions of people on the Internet, and an equal number of resources. Chances are good that someone else out there shares the same interests that you do.

The information you are looking for can come in many forms: searchable databases, ongoing private and public discussions, real-time chat sessions, electronic mail, and others. The Internet is truly multimedia, delivering text, images, moving pictures, and sound to your computer.

WHO PUTS INFORMATION ON THE INTERNET?

Individuals who have something to say, businesses that have products or services to sell, organizations and government departments with information to share. Anyone with a computer and an Internet connection can make information available to the world.

WHY SHOULD I USE THE INTERNET?

Human resource professionals should use the Internet regularly because it can be a resource to help improve your overall organization's effectiveness and offers the following benefits:

Convenience

The Internet never closes, so you can "visit" anything you want 24 hours a day, 7 days a week. If you have a computer and modem at home or at the office, you can get the information you need by simply logging on. You don't even have to place job openings in the newspaper anymore. You can post job openings online, so candidates can browse employment opportunities at their own convenience.

Time

The Internet is being used to quickly gather timely information needed for making decisions affecting human resources in order to develop a more productive and competitive work force. You can search millions of files in seconds. By using features such as electronic mail, you can send messages and reply to the messages instantly and at your convenience. You do not have to wait for the mailman any more.

Money

The Internet saves you money. By using the electronic mail feature of the Internet, human resource professionals can send and receive messages at a small cost, compared to a long distance telephone call, fax, or overnight mail service. By having a Web site, you can also save printing and postage costs by offering prospective employees an application to complete online and send via e-mail.

Newsgroups

The Internet provides a number of unique ways to communicate with many professionals in the human resources field. One very popular way to communicate is USENET. USENET, short for Users Network, is the largest discussion forum in the world. It allows human resource managers with common interests to communicate with one another. You can search for discussion groups pertaining to specific topics, for example, groups on employment, workplaces, or career issues. **Misc.jobs.misc** would connect you to a discussion group that is specifically concerned with workplace issues.

Web Sites

The World Wide Web (commonly referred to as the Web) is a easy-to-use system that offers a vast amount of information. The Web consists of a huge collection of documents called Web pages, stored on computers around the world.

The opening page of a Web site is known as the "home page." The home page is usually found at the address that you use to access a particular organization's site. A home page serves as a table of contents to the information that is provided at a particular Web site.

There are also links that can be used to connect directly to the other related pages at a Web site.

Online Services

A commercial online service can provide you access to the Internet for a fee. Well-known commercial online services include American Online, CompuServe, Microsoft Network, and Prodigy.

Commercial online services are easy to set up and usually provide a good customer support for questions you may have.

Communications

You can exchange electronic mail (e-mail) with human resources people around the world. E-mail is the most widely used feature on the Internet.

E-mail is much faster than first-class mail sent through the U.S. Postal Service. A message can travel around the world in seconds. A message can contain a few lines of text or several hundred. And unlike the postal service, there is no charge for sending and receiving electronic mail, even if the message travels around the world. Why spend money on long distance calls when you can save money by using the Internet to exchange messages.

Networking

Human resource professionals can make many new contacts who have information and influence. Think of the networking possibilities with all the HR personnel on the Internet.

For human resource professionals, the traditional methods of networking to find the right employee to hire can be tedious, expensive and frustrating. You call up someone you've never met before and mention that you're a friend of a friend. You might even have to fly to meet people to network with.

Everybody knows someone on the Internet. Diversity of the Internet audience is a great reason to job hunt online. True, not everyone you meet online will be a corporate recruiter, but someone you meet online or through newsgroups might know someone else who is looking for an employee just like you to hire.

Some people say "It's not what you know, it's who you know." The truth is that it's both, and you can definitely use both in searching for the right candidate to hire or in your own Internet job search.

HOW DO I FIND HUMAN RESOURCES INFORMATION ON THE WORLD WIDE WEB?

The fastest-growing part of the Internet is the World Wide Web, so it's not surprising that there are many different tools for searching it. Some Web cataloging resources are "search-oriented." You can enter keywords, and the program will look for sites that match your needs.

Others are "topic-oriented," meaning they let you navigate a series of menus until you find the information you want. Searching works well if you are looking for a very specific topic, but browsing by topic is often better if you aren't quite sure what you're looking for, or if you're just "cruising" for whatever catches your eye.

Tools for searching the Web include AltaVista, Lycos, WebCrawler, and Excite.

The Internet's best-known tool for searching the Web is Yahoo. Yahoo lists fewer sites than other resources, but is very well organized.

Another service, InfoSeek allows searches of Web pages, newsgroups and computer databases unavailable elsewhere.

How Do I Search Human Resource Newsgroups?

USENET, the "bulletin board of the Internet," is an enormous set of public discussion forums. With more than 15,000 separate newsgroups and more than 300 MB of new information posted every day, USENET is an incredible information warehouse. You can read newsgroups using newsreader software.

When you're looking for information on a specific subject and you don't know what newsgroup it is in, you can use a USENET searching tool to sort through the maze and pull out just the information you need. One such tool is called DejaNews. Another is SIFT, the Stanford Information Filtering Tool.

What is FTP?

Looking for a particular file on the Internet? If you use the Internet's File Transfer Protocol (FTP) tool, you already know that you can download the latest shareware and public domain utilities and applications for your computer. Perhaps you already know about the vast archives of picturers, sound and music files, and electronic books available through anonymous FTP.

If you've used anonymous FTP, you have probably also had trouble finding what you're looking for. FTP is a wonderful tool, a way to share hundreds of gigabytes of good stuff with the rest of the world. But because there are so many FTP sites, whose contents are usually arranged and indexed in a manner that would make a librarian cry, it's not particularly easy to find things through FTP.

What is Archie?

Archie is a program you can use to search for files at anonymous FTP sites. All you need to know is a file's name (or part of it), and Archie can point you to the file's FTP site, directory, and exact file name.

Although it does an admirable job of letting you search for files based on files names, you can't use Archie to search for programs based on what they do. Archie does not know how to ignore old versions of software. Archie won't just tell you where to find the latest version of a particular program, it will list all occurrences of that program, so you'll have to sift through them yourself.

What About Gopher and Veronica?

Although the Web is a great place to start an Internet information search, there are other resources on the Internet that you might want to explore. Most of the previously mentioned search tools don't adequately index "Gopherspace."

Gopher was the first program to make navigating the Internet truly easy for nontechnical users. Rather than having to TELNET or FTP to dozens of different sites in search of information (and remember all of those site names), Gopher is a menu-oriented tool for navigating the Internet. It presents you with lists of files, programs, resources, and services in the form of easy-to-read, point-and-click menus. You can navigate around Gopherspace by simply picking an item from a menu.

However, even the finest libraries are useless without a method for indexing their contents. Gopher's searching power comes from Veronica, a tool that is available from within Gopher. Veronica is an acronym for Very Easy Rodent-Oriented Net-wide Index to Computerized Archives. It is a system that indexes the entire set of Gopher menus available worldwide and lets you quickly search for specific information throughout Gopherspace. Unlike the World Wide Web, which has many choices for searching, Veronica is the de facto standard for searching Gopher space, and is a great starting point for almost any information search.

To use Veronica, you need to use Gopher to find a "Veronica gateway," usually a menu item that says "Search Gopherspace using Veronica."

WHAT DOES URL MEAN?

URL is an acronym for Universal Resource Locator. The Internet Engineering Task Force (IETF) originally designed the URL to be a standard code for addressing Internet sites. A URL is similar to a physical street address. It is a simple one-line code that directs a node on the Internet to a particular site.

A URL is composed of two to five distinct parts separated from one another by specific characters. The structure of a URL looks like this:

protocol://host name:port number/directory path/file name

The protocol refers to the Internet resource type, such as ***http***, which indicates Hypertext Transport Protocol, or the World Wide Web; ***ftp*** represents "file"; telnet; news (for pointing to a newsgroup). The protocol code must be followed by a colon (***:***) and often by double forward slashes (***//***) as well.

The host name refers to a specific Internet server, such as ***www.jobcenter.com***. The host name is made up of two or more parts, separated by periods(***.***).

The last part of the host name denotes the Internet domain, which indicates the type of Internet service and the country code of the server's physical location. The domain types include ***.com*** (typically a business or commercial organization), ***.edu*** (an educational institution), ***.gov*** (a government entity), ***.mil*** (a military service), ***.net*** (a gateway, administrative network host, or Internet Service Provider), and ***.org*** (usually a public service or nonprofit organization).

In addition, each country has its own top-level domain. For example, the ***.us*** domain represents the United States; however, it is often excluded from a URL. Other countries represented by domains include Canada (***.ca***), the United Kingdom (***.uk***), and Japan (***.jp***).

The code of a particular URL must be entered exactly, character for character, in order to access the correct site on the Internet. Some systems are case sensitive, so pay attention to lowercase and capital letters. For more information, refer to the World Wide Web Consortium's guide to URLs and Internet addressing schemes at ***http://www.w3/org/hyptertext/Addressing/Addressing.html***.

WHAT IS A MAILING LIST?

A mailing list (also called an e-mail discussion list) is a type of discussion forum that takes place in electronic mail. When you send your comments to the mailing list's e-mail address, your message is transmitted to a group of people rather than an individual. It is similar to USENET in that users can participate in discussions of thousands of topics. However, mailing list messages are delivered via electronic mail rather than read using a specialized client as with USENET.

A user can subscribe to a mailing list discussion by sending a subscription request e-mail to a special address. To stop receiving messages from the mailing list, the user must unsubscribe from the list. The e-mail address that you must send your request to is almost always different than the addresses of the list itself. If you send a subscription or unsubscription request to the list itself rather than the administrative address, your message will be forwarded to everyone on the list, annoying them all.

Mailing lists are somewhat more private than newsgroups. To read a mailing list, you must actively send a subscription request to a person or computer program. This alone discourages the wanton "lurking" that is common in newsgroups. Many mailing lists are open to the public, but some are not; they can be "by invitation only" or open to only members of a specific organization. Unlike newsgroups, unwanted or disruptive individuals can be excluded from the forum. For these reasons, mailing lists are commonly used to create smaller, more private communities than newsgroups provide.

Some mailing lists are huge. There is nothing to prevent a popular mailing list from growing to hundreds or thousands of subscribers. A disadvantage of subscribing to a popular mailing list is that your electronic mailbox can be flooded with dozens of messages each day.

HOW DO I SEND ELECTRONIC MAIL TO HR PROFESSIONALS ON ONLINE SERVICES?

To send mail to a subscriber of an online service you subscribe to, you often need only type the user name of that colleague. Sending e-mail from your Internet account to other Human Resources professionals who use other online services is straightforward. You need two pieces of information: your colleague's user name, and the name of the system that he or she uses.

- To send to America Online: **username@aol.com**. Use all lowercase letters and remove spaces. For example, username "Net Answers" becomes **netanswers@aol.com**.
- To send to CompuServe: **userid@compuserve.com**. Use the numeric CompuServe identification number, but use a period instead of a comma to separate the number sets. For example, to send mail to CompuServe user 1770,101, use the address **1770.101@compuserve.com**.
- To send to Microsoft Network use the form: **username @msn.com**.
- To send to Prodigy: **userid@prodigy.com**. The user ID is a combination of letters and numbers, like BVXF64A.

HOW CAN I USE THE INTERNET TO TALK WITH OTHER HUMAN RESOURCES PROFESSIONALS?

When you are logged on to the Internet, you can "talk" with other people who are logged on at the same time. Talking is different than exchanging e-mail messages. E-mail is analogous to sending paper mail through the postal service, while Internet talk is more like speaking to someone directly over the telephone or engaging in a conference call. It is instantaneous and requires two or more participants to be logged on simultaneously.

There are several methods of talking with your associates. Depending on your computer equipment, communications access, and personal preferences, you can choose from a growing variety of Internet chat applications. Two popular ways to conduct a text-based conversation are Internet Relay Chat (IRC) and Netscape Chat.

CHAPTER 3

HOW DO I GET STARTED?

CHAPTER 3

HOW DO I GET STARTED?

WHAT DO I NEED?

The requirements for accessing the Internet fall into three categories: equipment, a telephone line, and an account with an Internet Service Provider. A few other issues, including what protocols and browsers to use, should also be taken into consideration.

EQUIPMENT REQUIREMENTS

Hooking up to the Internet is rather simple. However, you must have the right equipment. You only need three pieces of equipment to start surfing:

- A computer,
- Lots of memory, and
- A modem.

Chances are you already have a computer on your desk. Whether its an IBM-compatible or Macintosh machine, you can use it to access the Internet. Pentium machines put you in the Internet fast lane, but a 286, 386 or 486 computer will get you to your destination.

Memory

You may need additional memory to accomodate the software necessary to access your ISP and to download files from the Web. Many entry-level computers come with four megabytes of random access memory (RAM), but 8 megabytes is the minimum needed to run most World Wide Web browsers smoothly. Sixteen megabytes would be better.

Modems

WHAT KIND OF MODEM DO I NEED?

In brief, a fast one. The term modem is an abbreviation of modulator-demodulator. It is a computer accessory that allows your computer to communicate with other computers over telephone lines. If your computer does not have an internal modem, you can either have an internal modem installed or purchase an external model.

Because the modem will be your link to the Internet, it's important to get the fastest model your computer can support. With a fast modem, images and text will snap up onto your screen, while a slow modem will give you plenty of time to make a pot of coffee while you wait.

What does "fast" mean in the modem world? Modems are rated by the number of bits per second (bps) the modem can transmit. A high speed modem can quickly pay for itself in telephone and connection charge savings. When buying a modem, be careful to read the fine print. Some fax modems handle faxes at 9,600 bps, but data at only 4,800 bps. It is the data rate that saves you money.

Modems, like computers, have undergone a rapid evolution. A 33,600 bps modem (called a "thirty-three-six") costs under $200. Resist the temptation to make do with a slower modem: the difference between a 14,400-bps modem and one running at 28,800 is more noticeable than you might think. A few online services still offer 14,400 as their highest access speed, but eventually they'll all switch to 28,800 (and in the meantime, your 28,800 modem will work perfectly well at the slower speed). U.S. Robotics, Hayes, Supra, and Motorola are the top modem manufacturers.

If you're using an older computer, it's important to check whether it can support one of the new fast modems. Because of the configuration of their communications ports, some older machines may be unable to support speeds of more than 9,600 or 14,400 bps, so check your user's manual. If this is the case with your computer, buy the fastest modem your machine will support.

TELEPHONE LINES

You should have a dedicated phone line for your computer. If you use your existing phone line for Internet access, keep in mind that anyone who tries to reach you while you're online will get a busy signal. Don't let the phone company tell you that you need a special data line for a modem—you don't.

If you have problems with the line you use with your computer (especially excessive line noise, which can seriously degrade throughput, or data transfer speed), tell the phone company service reps that you use the line for a fax machine. They seem to understand fax/phone problems better than computer/phone glitches.

ISDN

High-speed digital, or ISDN (Integrated Services Digital Network) lines will double or triple traditional phone line data transfer speeds. ISDN service is already available from phone companies in many areas, although the price of such connections is still rather high for all but the most dedicated Internet users.

Unlike plain old telephone service (POTS), ISDN is a digital telephone standard, giving phone users noise-free lines, and can be used for Internet access (as long as there's a local Internet Service Provider who's providing ISDN connections).

What so important about ISDN? Simple: speed. An ISDN line gives you at least a 64 Kbps connection, approximately five times as fast as the modems most people use. Graphics download more quickly, making the experience of browsing the Web a real pleasure. In addition, there is no wait while your computer dials the service provider—the connection is almost instantaneous.

ISDN SERVICES

What You Need
- An ISDN adapter for your computer.
- TCP/IP support for your computer.

The Pluses
- Faster than a speeding modem! ISDN connections are available at speeds of 64 Kbps and 128 Kbps.
- Connection (unlike some commercial providers) is instantaneous.
- You can run graphical Web browsers like Netscape.
- You can download files directly to your computer.

The Minuses
- ISDN telephone services charges are higher than plain old telephone service (POTS).
- ISDN is not available in all areas.

INTERNET ACCESS

ONLINE SERVICES VERSUS INTERNET SERVICE PROVIDERS

Once you have the equipment and phone line you need to connect to the online world, the next step is to find a service provider. There are many different types of service providers, offering different levels of access to the Internet.

Obtaining commercial Internet access is usually just a matter of choosing between two principal alternatives: the large national online services or local Internet Service Providers.

The big four (as they are known in the online world), CompuServe, America Online, Prodigy, and Microsoft Network, currently provide Internet access to roughly half the people using the Web.

If you want to use any of the four major commercial online services, you will pay a monthly fee that's comparable to what an independent Internet Service Provider would charge. Until you become more familiar with the Net, you will probably prefer the convenience and support an online service provides, as opposed to the 'you're on your own' approach offered by smaller ISPs.

ONLINE SERVICES

Online services, such as America Online, CompuServe, Prodigy, and Microsoft Network have become so visible in popular culture that an introduction seems unnecessary.

Commercial online services can give you access to the Internet for a fee. They offer information that is well organized, such as news, weather reports and financial information. They're easy to use.

When you join one of the major online services, they will charge you a flat monthly fee, usually under $20.00 per month for unlimited usage.

America Online

Not only does AOL have the largest number of members, it provides the best Internet access of all the online services. One of the key reasons: The firm's nationwide 28.8 Kbps access by means of the AOL network. If you're not near one of AOL's points of presence (places where you can dial a local phone number to log on), you can use AOL's nationwide 800 access.

America Online, Inc.
8619 Westwood Center Drive
Vienna, VA 22182

800-827-6364
703-448-8700
www.aol.com

What You Need

- A 14.4 Kbps (preferably 28.8 Kbps) modem.
- AOL's Windows or Macintosh software.
- An AOL subscription.

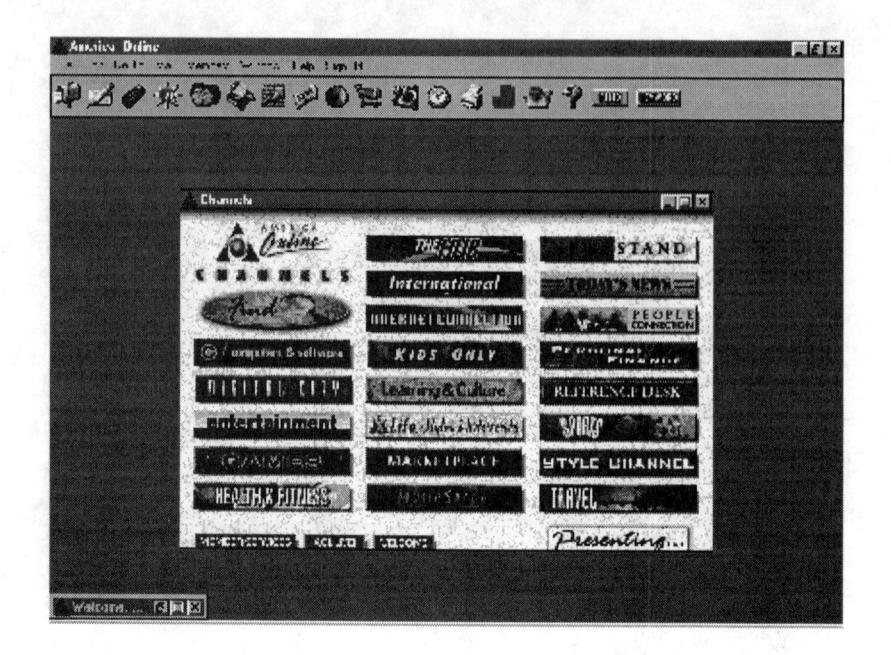

The Pluses

- You can run any Web browser, including Netscape (Windows version only).
- Installation and configuration are automatic.
- 28.8 Kbps access is widely available.
- Free additional e-mail addresses.

The Minuses

- 28.8 Kbps access may not be available in your area.
- Macintosh support lags behind Windows support.

CompuServe

One of the oldest of the computer online services, Compuserve (now known as CSi) has run behind the other online services in offering Web browsing capabilities. Still, after acquiring Internet software company Spry, CompuServe has made a determined effort to catch-up.

How Do I Get Started?

CompuServe, Inc.
5000 Arlington Centre Blvd.
PO Box 20212
Columbus, OH 43220

800-848-8199
614-718-2800

www.compuserve.com

What You Need

- A 14.4 Kbps (preferably 28.8 Kbps) modem.
- CompuServe's Windows or Macintosh software.
- A CompuServe subscription.

The Pluses

- You can run any Web browser, including Netscape (Windows version only).
- Installation and configuration are easy (28.8 Kbps access is widely available.
- Free additional e-mail addresses.

The Minuses

- 28.8 Kbps access may not be available in your area.
- Macintosh support lags behind Windows support.

The Microsoft Network

If you're using Windows 95, this option may very well provide you with the best possible means of accessing the Internet. It's beautifully integrated with Windows 95—too beautifully, according to Microsoft's competitors—so it's a snap to subscribe.

Microsoft Network Services
Microsoft Corporation
One Microsoft Way
Redmond, WA 98052

800-373-3676
206-882-8080

www.msn.com

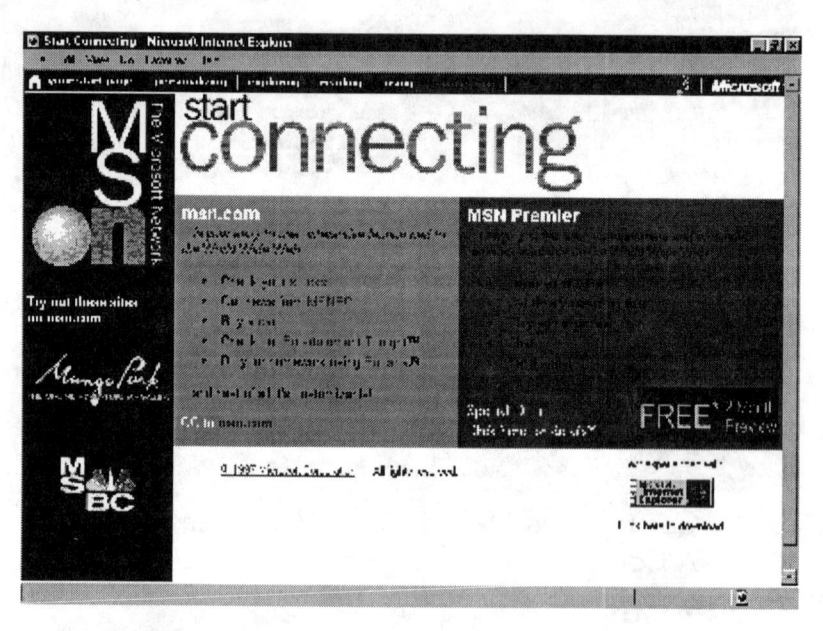

What You Need

- A 14.4 Kbps (preferably 28.8 Kbps) modem.
- Windows 95.
- A subscription to the Microsoft Network.

The Pluses

- You can run use Microsoft's capable Internet Explorer browser, or any other browser, including Netscape.
- Installation and configuration are automatic.

How Do I Get Started?

- 28.8 Kbps access is available, but not as widely available as AOL and CompuServe.
- Free additional e-mail addresses.

The Minuses

- MSN's internal content is sparse in comparison to AOL and CompuServe.
- Available only for users of Windows 95.
- 28.8 Kbps access may not be available in your area.

Prodigy

The first of the major online services to offer a Web browser, Prodigy offers an integrated Web browser. Unlike AOL and CompuServe, though, Prodigy has some serious drawbacks for would-be Web surfers at present. At this books writing, though, Prodigy was planning to license Netscape Navigator, which should make it a major contender (if you're willing to put up with the 14.4 Kbps access, that is).

Prodigy Services Corporation
445 Hamilton Ave
White Plains, NY 10601

800-776-3449
914-448-8000
www.prodigy.com

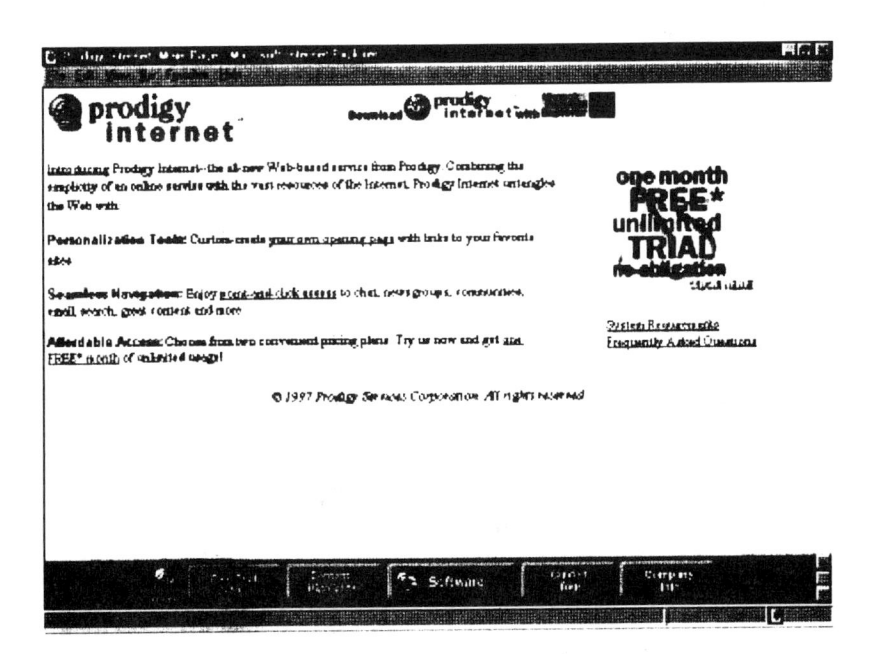

What You Need
- A 14.4 Kbps modem.
- Prodigy's Windows or Macintosh software.
- A Prodigy subscription.

The Pluses
- If you are using Windows, you can use Netscape Navigator to access Prodigy.
- Installation and configuration are automatic.

The Minuses
- The fastest supported connection is 14.4 Kbps.
- The browser can't handle many of the advanced features you'll find on the Web today.
- The service won't currently allow you to use other browsers besides the one built into its interface.

Which Service is Right for You?

The pros and cons of subscribing to one of these online services are the topic of endless debate, but several points in favor of using them are worth noting, especially if you are a newcomer to the online word.

Each of these services has a great deal of content, features that are not available on the Net as a whole. Each offers a particular selection of newspapers and magazines, and several devote substantial space to book discussion groups, etc. Your best bet is to check the publicity material for each service or enroll in a trial account. If something one of them carries strikes you as important, go ahead and subscribe.

These services have prospered by making getting online a painless, non-threatening experience, even for the most technically inexperienced user. If it's comforting to know that technical help is just a phone call away any day of the week, you may want to go this route.

Recognizing that the Internet can sometimes be a confusing place for newcomers, all of these services have devoted a great deal of effort to making the jump from the cozy security of their service into the Internet as easy as possible. Help files and tips on everything from how to behave on the Net to how to find a particular site are offered to every customer. Anyone who actually reads all the informational materials these services offer their users before they access the Net will know more about the Net than many people who have used the Internet for years.

All of these services offer free trial accounts, usually 10 or 15 free hours, in which to check out what the service has to offer. Getting a free trial account usually involves giving the service credit card information so that billing can begin as soon as your free time is used up, but such trial accounts can be a good way to choose a service that you really enjoy.

All in all, a major online service is probably a good way to check out the Net and decide whether to proceed to a more direct connection. If you decide that you really like browsing the offerings of one particular service for just a few hours every month, fine. Millions of people are happy doing just that. However, if you decide after a few months that the lure of the wide-open Net is too strong to resist, a flat-fee independent Internet access provider is in your future.

INTERNET SERVICE PROVIDERS

The last couple of years have seen the emergence of an alternative to the major online services. Independent Internet Service Providers (ISPs) sell access to the Internet. Customers dial into an ISP via a modem, and the ISP connects to the Net. Connecting to the Internet through an ISP has several advantages over connection through online services like America Online, Prodigy, CompuServe and Microsoft.

ISPs are almost always cheaper than the larger on-line services. A simple shell (text-only) account with an ISP costs about $10.00 per month for unlimited connection time.

Another advantage of ISPs is that they almost always provide faster, easier access to the Internet than do the online services. And ISPs generally carry a full USENET newsfeed, meaning that the user can access any news group they choose.

Basics

Your Internet provider is your link to the Internet. There are a few basic services your Internet Service Provider (ISP) must provide.

- A Well Maintained Network: When you connect with your ISP, you become part of their network. Your ability to communicate across the Net will depend on your ISP's network capabilities.
- Available Phone Lines: Your ISP must have enough lines to match the demand for their service. All lines should be capable of 28.8 Kbps.
- They Should Provide You with the Basic Tools Necessary to Get Online: This includes connection software, a WWW browser, e-mail, a newsgroup reader, and an Internet chat package.
- Available and Competent Technical Support: Your provider should offer support during peak hours of operation. The support staff should be able to answer all basic questions regarding the components of the Internet as well as handle difficult connection problems.
- Provide Help Files, Links, Search Capabilities and Other Services from Their Home Page: Many Internet Service Providers only offer an Internet connection point. Your enjoyment of the Internet can be greatly enhanced by the right Internet Service Provider.

Connections

Dedicated (permanent) connections are high speed lines connected to host computers that are permanently online, 24-hours a day. Used by large companies, corporations and universities that can afford the $10,000+ annual fees. If your organization is connected, you might be able to obtain free access using their dedicated line.

E-mail connections are the first level of access, allowing only e-mail messages to be sent to other users on the Internet.

How Do I Get Started?

A Dial-up Terminal Emulation (shell) account works as follows: Your modem dials up and links up to a service provider's computer that is connected to the Internet, and uses the terminal emulation feature in the communications software to handle large data transfers.

With a Dial-up Direct Connection, also called a Dial-up Serial Line Internet Protocol (SLIP)/Point-to-Point Protocol (PPP) account, your modem dials a server host computer and becomes directly connected to the Internet. Your computer them has its own Internet Protocol (IP) address. In effect, you contract with a service for a dedicated line for a period of time, but for a lot less money than a dedicated connection.

Pricing

What types of access subscription plans are available? Hourly and unlimited access plans are available, often from the same provider. CompuServe and America Online, like many local ISPs also charge a flat monthly rate for personal accounts, including unlimited access time. Since the monthly charges for both online services and ISPs are constantly changing, price information for individual services has been deliberately left out of this book.

Going It Alone

You should be aware that in opting for an ISP, you're giving up the buffer between the Net and yourself that an online service provides. When you connect to an ISP, there is nothing there—no welcome screen, no helpful tips, and no online customer service department hovering at your elbow, waiting to lead you on a guided tour of the Net. You're simply connected to the Internet in all its glorious chaos. This can be a disconcerting experience for novices. On the other hand, keep in mind that many reputable ISPs have a help line that you can call with your questions.

Setting up a SLIP/PPP connection can be more complicated than installing the software for an online service. Typically, your new ISP will provide you with disks containing a TCP/IP dialer. Setting up the TCP/IP dialer can be a bit tricky. If you're brand-new to computers or modems, make sure that the ISP you choose is willing to walk you through the process of setting up. Any reputable ISP will be glad to help.

On-line Advice on Choosing An ISP

Depending on where you live, you'll have your choice of anywhere from one to 20 local ISPs plus several national providers. There are good providers and bad providers. Word of mouth is probably your best clue. If you already have access to the Internet (via an online service or a friend), the best places to find information and opinions about Internet Service Providers are the Usenet newsgroups **alt.internet.services**, **alt.internet.access.wanted** and **alt.online.services**. If you have a question about a specific provider, just post it to one of these groups, and chances are you'll get an earful, both pro and con.

If you have access to the World Wide Web, there's a very handy Web page called The List at **http://www.thelist.com**, which includes nearly all the ISPs in the world, organized by country and area code. Entries for the providers include area codes served, services offered, prices, and telephone numbers. A few minutes spent browsing The List will probably produce at least one likely candidate.

Other Resources for Choosing a Provider

If you have no Net access yet, your best bet for finding a local or regional ISP will probably be a quick search of newspaper ads and local bookstores. There are several directories of Internet Service Providers available.

Another possibility would be to contact a national service provider such as Netcom (800-353-6600), that offers SLIP/PPP connections in most areas of the United States.

Still another possible avenue for finding an ISP would be to invest in one of the ready-made Internet access kits, such as Internet in a Box, sold in computer software stores and some bookstores. These kits include the software for basic Internet applications (dialing program, World Wide Web browser, e-mail program, etc.) as well as a free trial offer (usually 10 hours or so of online time) with a national Internet service provider.

If you decide to try one of these kits, make sure that the software can be used with any ISP, not just the one offering the free trial. Although your first few hours on-line with the kit's chosen service provider may be free, dialing into the provider may be a long-distance call for you, which takes most of the fun out of "free". It's possible, even if accessing the provider is via a local call, that you will consistently get busy signals when you try to dial into the system. But if you first verify that the software can be used with any provider, you can use that free time to find a provider closer to home or less overloaded and switch to it as soon as possible.

The proliferation of local Internet Service Providers is starting to affect the plans of the large online services. Recognizing the superiority of a SLIP/PPP connection over the old-style dial-up hookup, several of the large online services are now offering special TCP/IP arrangements that allow users to dial into the service, then run third-party Internet applications such as Netscape along side the service's proprietary software.

The large online services have decided to give the small local ISPs a run for their money by offering their own bare-bones Internet-only services. America Online, CompuServe, and Prodigy have all established national TCP/IP networks providing full Internet access at rates substantially lower than each service's "full-featured" online offerings. Information on these services can be obtained from the phone numbers listed above. While this sort of account is still usually more expensive than a connection to a local ISP, it may be an option for you if you live in an area without any ISPs at all. These services' nationwide networks of access numbers make this kind of account an especially attractive option for frequent travelers.

Not to be outdone by the online services, both AT&T and MCI now offer Internet access for a low monthly fee, and will soon be joined in the Internet-access business by other national and regional telephone service providers.

The good new is that, with so much competition in the field, prices for Net access are almost certain to fall in the near future. On the other hand, the volatility of the market means that no guide, not even this one, can keep pace with all the new options for Internet access.

PHONE COMPANIES GET INTO THE ACT

It's not surprising that the major telecommunications companies are becoming ISPs. They have the phone lines and nationwide transmission system, not to mention name-brand recognition among consumers.

Internet MCI

Internet MCI is designed for the millions of computer users who have installed high-speed modems in their personal computers. Aided by point-and-click software, users can quickly install the necessary computer programs, which include Netscape's highly regarded Web browser, Netscape Navigator. Phone: 800-550-0927.

www.internetmci.com

AT&T World Net Services

AT&T is working with Netscape to provide online services that will include e-mail and an extensive directory to find places, resources and people on the Internet. Phone: 800-831-5259.

www.att.com/worldnet

OTHER SELECTION CONSIDERATIONS

Protocols

Dialup IP lets computer users achieve a direct connection to the Internet by using a modem and telephone line. IP is short for Internet Protocols. Dialup IP enables your computer to communicate directly with the Internet. The keys to this direct Internet connectivity are SLIP and PPP, the two most widely-used protocols (standards) for connecting computers to the Internet by means of dialup connections.

The principal advantage of having a SLIP/PPP connection is speed. The difference between visiting a Web page via one of the online service web browsers and seeing the same page snap up on your screen in Netscape is amazing, making the Internet a more enjoyable place to visit.

SLIP and CSLIP

SLIP stands for Serial Line Interface Protocol, one of the older Internet protocols. SLIP establishes the procedure that sends Internet data through your modem and plain old telephone service (POTS) lines. To be directly connected to the Internet, you computer needs an Internet Protocol (IP) address, a unique numerical address required of every computer directly connected to the Internet. The service provider's computer assigns a unique IP address to each incoming SLIP line it handles.

Compressed SLIP (CSLIP) is a variation of SLIP that improves the performance of Internet applications that generate large amounts of small packets. You should use CSLIP if your access provider and your TCP/IP software support it.

PPP

PPP, or Point-to-Point Protocol, is a more recent Internet standard governing the transfer of Internet data via modems and telephone lines. Like SLIP, PPP generally involves a dynamically assigned (temporary) IP address, allowing exchanging Internet data with other Internet computers. But PPP is more up to date, offering data compression, data negotiation, and error correction to make the connection work more smoothly.

Which is better: SLIP or PPP?

The best dialup IP method is the one you can get. If you are lucky enough to have a choice, choose PPP because it offers automatic negotiation of such things as IP addresses.

SLIP/PPP Services

What you need

- A high-speed modem (at least 14.4Kbps).

- TCP/IP support for your computer.
- SLIP/PPP software.
- A SLIP, CSLIP, or PPP subscription to an Internet Service Provider.

The Pluses
- You can run graphical Web browsers such as Netscape on your computer.
- You can run other Internet programs, such as electronic mail, Gopher, or Archie at the same time.
- You can download files directly to your computer.

The Minuses
- SLIP/PPP accounts are more expensive.
- Installation can be a problem if the service provider does not provide you with reconfigured access software—insist on it!

WEB BROWSERS

To Buy or Not to Buy?

Web browsers are software programs that are used to find and view information on the Internet and World Wide Web. Most of the information you'll see on the Web is organized in linked hypertext pages. A page usually has colored or underlined text or graphics (linked to URL Web addresses) that you click on to bring up another page.

Netscape's Navigator and Microsoft Internet Explorer are two examples of the more than 25 multimedia browsers available. Usually one or more browsers are included in your Internet Service Provider's software, but you are not limited to using any particular one. Currently, Netscape Navigator is the most popular browser, but Microsoft Internet Explorer is gaining acceptance. The next version of Netscape's browser, called Netscape Communicator, will team the browser with other desktop features.

Before shopping for any Web browser, take a look at what is already on your computer. If you purchased a computer in the last year that came with Windows 95 pre-installed, you probably have a copy of Microsoft's Internet Explorer on your system.

NETSCAPE NAVIGATOR

Netscape Navigator, is without question, the leading Web browser today. Approximately seven out of every ten people who use the Web are using Netscape. It's faster than the other browsers, is loaded with features, and is available in Microsoft Windows and Macintosh versions.

Netscape is fast, efficient, easy to install and configure, and fun to use. It displays graphics faster than any other browser on the market. Businesses and government organizations may download a copy and use Netscape free for 90 days to evaluate the product. If you decide to purchase a copy, it sells for $49.00. Netscape is free for students, faculty and staff of educational institutions.

Some of the features of Netscape's browser are:

- E-mail: Netscape comes with a very good built-in e-mail program that lets you send, receive and organize electronic mail.
- USENET: Netscape has an easy-to-use and powerful USENET newsreader.
- Plug-Ins: Plug-Ins are accessory programs that expand on an application's capabilities. Netscape includes a Virtual Reality Modeling Language (VRML) reader, a program that enables users to read spreadsheets embedded into Web pages. This new capability is far beyond what other browsers currently offer.
- Frames: Frames lets Web page creators break a page into two or more independently scrollable panes. This also keeps navigation buttons in view.

Netscape has a very nice status bar at the bottom of the display. The status bar lets you determine exactly what the browser is doing at any given moment, including the percentage of the current Web page and its graphics that have downloaded to your computer. Although this information may not be terribly useful, it does help keep impatient users at ease, showing how much time is left to complete the download.

It also features an excellent bookmarking system that enables users to set up bookmark lists anyway they want. This feature is invaluable if you spend any serious amount of

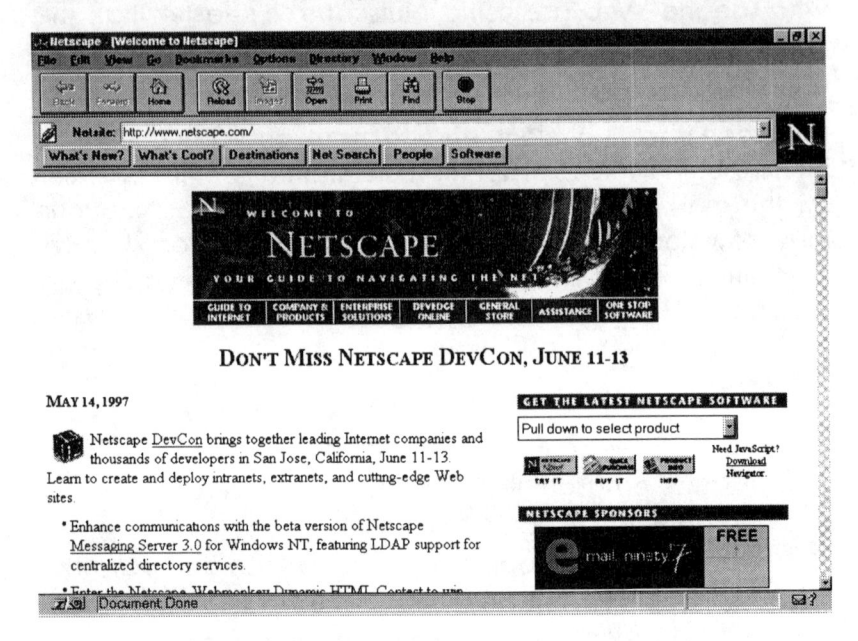

time on the Web. You can keep bookmarks of favorite Web sites much like a bookmark holds the page in a book you're reading.

Another nice feature of Navigator is the capability to make notes on each site, for when you are trying to remember exactly what it was that previously interested you about that site.

MICROSOFT INTERNET EXPLORER

Microsoft did not realize that the Internet was the "next big market" until very recently. One of the best things about Microsoft's browser is the hassle-free way that the program works with sounds, videos, and other Web sources. without installing any add-on applications.

How Do I Get Started?

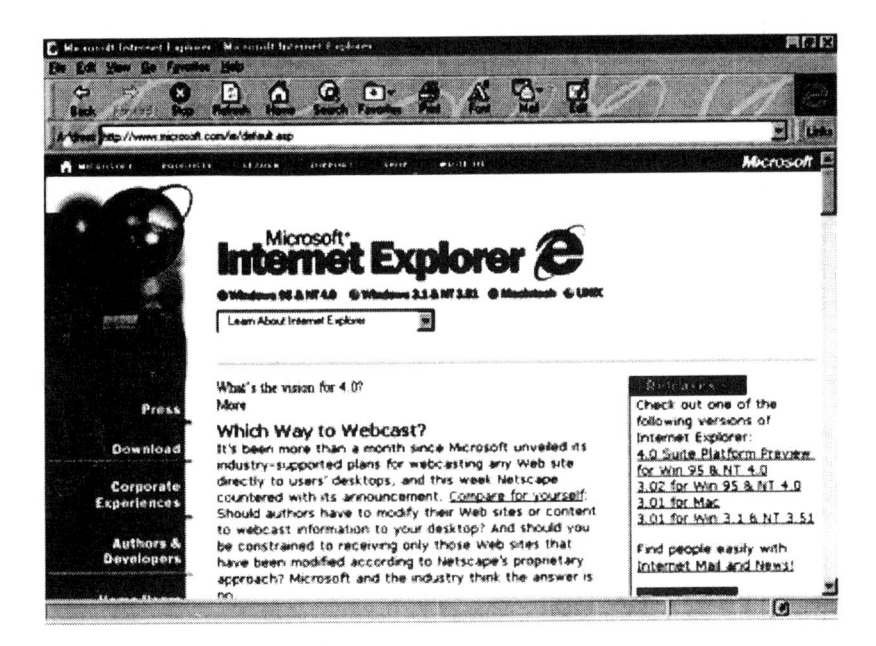

Internet Explorer is available for Windows 95, Windows 3.1, Windows NT and the Macintosh. You can download a copy of the Internet Explorer from Microsoft's Web site at **http://www.microsoft.com** and use it for free.

Although Internet Explorer lacks some of the features of Netscape's browser, including a full-feature newsreader and e-mail (although Windows 95 users might want to use Microsoft Exchange as their e-mail program), Internet Explorer has an advantage over Netscape: every computer sold with Windows 95 on it includes a copy of Internet Explorer.

Some of Internet Explorer's features include:

- Resizeable toolbar: Provides quick links to World Wide Web pages.
- Separate download windows: Instead of waiting for a file to download, you can start a download in a separate window and continue surfing.
- Security: It includes the latest on-line features, making it safer than ever to send credit card information over the Internet.

CHAPTER 4
WHAT IS ELECTRONIC MAIL?

CHAPTER 4
WHAT IS ELECTRONIC MAIL?

THE MOST POPULAR ONLINE TOOL

If computers were more affordable, the US Postal Service would be much less busy.

Electronic mail is the application that was most responsible for the early growth of the Internet. Remember those researchers who were involved with the initial development of the Internet? They used e-mail to exchange ideas, information, and reports related to their scientific projects.

E-mail remains an extremely popular Internet application because it's a fast, economical, and easy way to send messages and files to anybody with an e-mail account. In fact, computer users have coined an interesting term for posting mail via the US Postal service—snail mail!

E-mail can be used to:
- Send single or multiple messages to individuals.
- Send single or multiple messages to several individuals at once, or to groups of individuals.
- Send text files.
- Send binary documents (such as spreadsheets or

graphics).
- Distribute electronic flyers, newsletters, and magazines.
- Broadcast notices or updates to groups of individuals.

It's Increasingly Popular

Electronic mail was the vehicle for an estimated 1.7 trillion messages in 1996. E-mail addresses are now commonly included on business cards, stationery, etc. Here's how e-mail message volume in 1996 compared with the grandfather of message transfer, the US Postal Service:

	E-mail	**Post Office**
Per Hour:	194 million	20.5 million
Per Day:	4.7 billion	493 million
Per Year:	1.7 trillion	180 billion

A human resource department can compose a single message and distribute it simultaneously to its Internet-connected staff worldwide. You can send messages to and receive messages from anyone anywhere in the world using e-mail. You can also attach and send, or receive, files containing text, graphic images, or even audio and video.

GETTING STARTED

To use e-mail, you need an account from an Internet access provider, e-mail software and a computer address. Eudora, SPRY, and Pegasus for Windows are common e-mail programs (there are e-mail programs for Windows and Macintosh operating platforms). When you subscribe to an Internet Service Provider, an e-mail program is usually included in your basic service. You are then assigned an e-mail address and can start corresponding via the Internet.

E-mail is changing the way people communicate. The parties on the receiving end do not have to be present at their computer when you send e-mail to them. (This is like an answering machine that takes telephone messages for you when you're not home.) Your message travels to the destination mailbox at the speed of light. But the person at the other end still has to check their mailbox to read your message!

E-mail Addresses

E-mail addresses typically look something like this:

hrexec@your_company.com

- **hrexec** is the individual's name as known to the local computer that collects and processes his or her e-mail. Typically, the user name is selected at the time of subscription.
- **your_company** represents the name of the computer that collects e-mail for the organization or service provider.
- **com** identifies the type of Internet user (in this case, a commercial business).

Some common "endings" and their meanings

com	commercial business (companies)
edu	education (universities and other educational organizations)
gov	government (non-military)
mil	US military or defense organizations
net	network operation and service organizations
org	miscellaneous organizations (non-profit and research organizations)

Sending E-Mail is Easy

You have an example of a typical e-mail window below. Just write your message below the header bar and click on the Send button—it's that simple. Your message is sent immediately and received within a few seconds via the Net!

There is usually no charge for sending and receiving electronic mail, even if it travels around the world. Rather than making long distance calls to colleagues, you can save time and money by using the Internet to exchange information.

For details on how to send mail from any network to any network, read the Inter-Network Mail Guide at ***ftp://ftp.csd.uwm.edu/pub/internetwork-mail-guide***. It

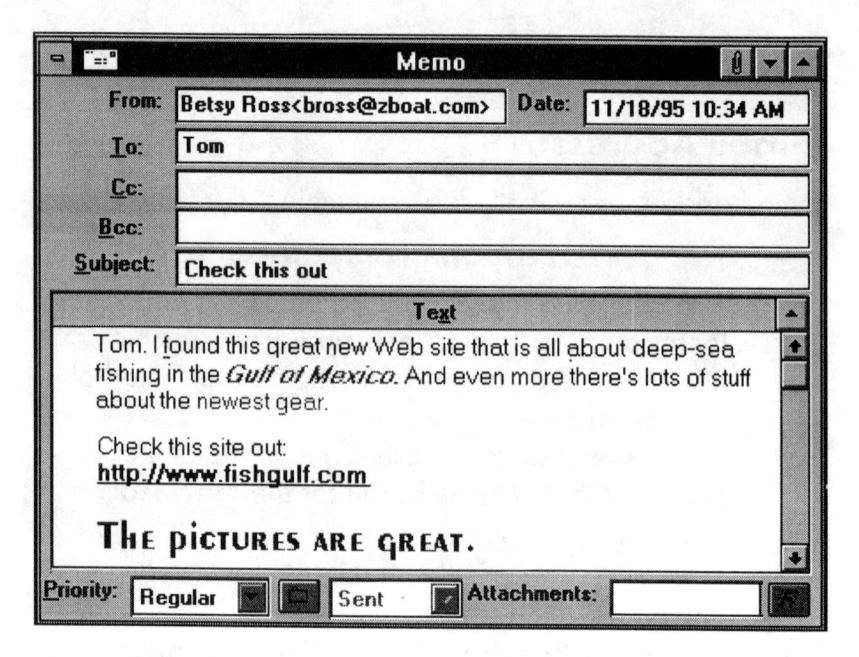

```
┌─────────────────────────────────────────────────────────┐
│ ─ ▣                        Memo                    ⊘ ▼ ▲│
│    From: │Betsy Ross<bross@zboat.com>│ Date: │11/18/95 10:34 AM│
│      To: │Tom                                          │
│      Cc: │                                             │
│     Bcc: │                                             │
│  Subject:│Check this out                               │
│ ────────────────── Text ──────────────────────────── ▲ │
│  Tom. I found this great new Web site that is all about deep-sea │
│  fishing in the Gulf of Mexico. And even more there's lots of stuff │
│  about the newest gear.                                │
│                                                        │
│  Check this site out:                                  │
│  http://www.fishgulf.com                               │
│                                                        │
│  THE piCTuREs ARE GREAT.                               │
│                                                      ▼ │
│ Priority: │Regular ▼│ ⊡ │ Sent ▼│ Attachments: │     │⇱│
└─────────────────────────────────────────────────────────┘
```

also tells how to send mail from networks other than the Internet.

E-Mail Software

Two of the most common E-mail programs for PCs running Windows are Eudora and Netscape Mail (which is built into the Netscape browser). Both are excellent programs. Eudora is fast, requires little storage space, and is easy to use. And because Netscape Mail is built in, you can browse the World Wide Web and have access to E-mail in one program.

There are two versions of Eudora, one that's free and one that's not. The free version is call Eudora Light (you can download a copy at ***http://www.eudora.com***). The registered version, Eudora Pro, has a lot more features, including a spell checker. You can buy it online at Qualcomm's Web site or at computer stores.

Organizing your e-mail is easy with these programs. They (and many others) have folders or "mail boxes" into which you can move incoming messages after you have read them. You also can put messages in a "trash" folder that will store your messages until you empty it.

For More Information, contact:

Eudora Pro
Qualcomm Inc.
(800) 233-3672/(619) 658-1291
www.eudora.com

Netscape Navigator/Communicator
Netscape Communications Corp.
(415) 937-2555
www.netscape.com

Types of E-Mail

The most common type of e-mail consists of plain text. Creating text e-mail is just like writing a letter. In fact, most e-mail programs will let you use your regular work processor to create the text, and then cut and paste it into a Send Box in the e-mail program. This is a good idea, because most programs don't have editing features, such as a spell checker. (The registered version of Eudora is an exception.)

E-mail is also a good way to distribute documents. You can easily attach files from most applications to an e-mail message when you send it. (Netscape Mail and the registered version of Eudora support attachments). You can attach images such as charts, graphs, and photographs scanned into your computer, even a company newsletter in a word processing format. When you attach a file to an e-mail, your program will package that file for data transmission.

If attaching files to your e-mail is important to you, make sure when you look for an e-mail program that it can support attachments. E-mail follows a standard for transferring files called Multi-purpose Internet Mail Extensions (MIME), a protocol that determines how different types of e-mail are packaged and how the packages are labeled electronically. Make sure the program you get can support MIME.

Technical Details

The packaging process splits data into packets with special tags called checksums and other data designed to repair a packet if it arrives with missing or incorrect data. If a packet arrives at its destination damaged, the receiving program will try to repair it, usually successfully. If it fails, it will warn you that the data is flawed and must be resent.

There are two major ways of packaging data: Uuencode (short for Unix-to-Unix, Encode), and Base64.

Uuencode is the older standard used during the early days of the Internet, when practically every computer on the Internet used the Unix operating system. When a file is Uuencoded, it typically grows by about 40 percent, including all the redundant information and checksums. The file is Uudecoded at its destination and shrinks to its original size.

Base64 takes up less space in transit, but not all e-mail programs are capable of decoding it upon arrival. If you receive an e-mail message with a Base64-encoded attachment, the program won't allow you to open the attached file, but will ask you to save the attachment in its encoded form as a file so that another program can decode it for you.

Finding E-mail Addresses

E-mail is a great way to inexpensively communicate with business associates—if you have their e-mail addresses.

One drawback to e-mail is that there are no comprehensive and accurate listings (like telephone directories) of everyone who has an e-mail address. Complicating matters is that computer users are opening and closing e-mail accounts and changing e-mail addresses all the time. Tracking down these addresses often involves calling to see if people have Internet access and if so, writing down their e-mail addresses.

Several sites on the World Wide Web provide search tools to help you find e-mail addresses. The Bigfoot Web site (**http://www.bigfoot.com**) maintains a list of about 8 million entries. Internet Address Finder (**http://www.iaf.net**) also has about 5 million entries. The Four11.com Web site (**http://www.four11.com**) uses phone numbers to find Internet addresses. There are other more-specialized e-mail directories as well. A good starting point to find e-mail address directories can be found at the Netscape Communications Corp. Web site (**http://**

home.netscape.com/escapes/whitepages/ people.html).

There are now ways to prevent the need to change e-mail addresses every time you move or close one account and open another. Some services are offer permanent e-mail addresses for free. For example, at the Bigfoot Web site, you can get a permanent e-mail address by simply providing a personal profile. You can then receive e-mail at ***<your name>@bigfoot.com*** and at your existing account. And free e-mail services such as Juno (***http://www.juno.com***) and the Web-based HotMail (***http//www.hotmail.com***) let you establish permanent e-mail addresses as long as you continue to subscribe to their services.

E-MAIL IS NO LAUGHING MATTER

Computer e-mail has become a blessing to corporate America, increasing staff communication and quickening the pace of information sharing. Unfortunately, some employees are using the medium to share unwanted racist or sexist messages.

In 1995, Chevron Corp. agreed to a $2.2 million settlement of a sexual-harassment suit after the plaintiffs presented e-mail records containing jokes which demeaned women. Recently, Morgan Stanley and R.R. Donnelley & Sons have been target of suits alleging that racist jokes were passed through the companies' e-mail systems, and Citicorp's Citibank division is facing an e-mail race-discrimination suit.

In the Citibank suit, two African-American employees allege that an e-mail message containing racist jokes was disseminated through the bank's e-mail system. Citicorp took disciplinary action against the individuals involved in "an incident regarding an e-mail that is contrary to Citicorp's policies about use of e-mail." One individual who had e-mail access but was no longer working for the company had severance benefits suspended, while others face termination, suspension without pay or revocation of pay increases.

One problem is that the kinds of inappropriate jokes that used to be shared in conversations at the water cooler are now being related in e-mail messages and preserved on hard drives, becoming evidence in employment-discrimination lawsuits.

Experts say e-mail users who electronically share racist or sexist jokes at work may not realize that these messages may be saved on their employer's computer systems. More companies should have formal policies about the proper uses of e-mail in order to protect themselves, these observers say.

Robert Rosell of Quality Media Recourses, a Bellevue, WA, company that teaches the legal and appropriate uses of e-mail, says "Where people get into trouble is where they confuse e-mail with a conversation. They say things in e-mail they would never say face-to-face to a person. That's what's leading a lot of people into trouble."

Companies have to accept the risk of liability from e-mail if they are to continue benefitting from the technology that has enabled them to boost their information-gathering capabilities. While some companies may be open to lawsuits, at least the new technology may help bring some improper behavior to light.

E-MAIL ETIQUETTE

What's the proper use of e-mail? To paraphrase Shakespeare, "Brevity is the soul of e-mail." Be action oriented and direct. Make your point in 30 words or less. As you read this, thousands of people throughout corporate America are unwittingly making or breaking jeopardizing important workplace relationships based on their choice of keystrokes in this seemingly innocuous communications medium.

IN FACT, SOME ARE UNINTENTIONALLY ANGERING COLLEAGUES BECAUSE THEY DON'T REALIZE THAT WRITING A MESSAGE IN CAPITAL LETTERS IS THE E-MAIL EQUIVALENT OF SHOUTING.

Widespread use of e-mail has spawned the need to educate users on its proper use. Here are some strategies for effective e-mail communication:

- Be brief: Reserve longer discussions for face-to-face or phone interaction.
- Be complete: Include the who, what, where, when, how and why to answer any anticipated questions.
- If you don't put your name on it, don't send it: Don't use e-mail (anonymous or otherwise) to say something you wouldn't say in person.
- Observe Netiquette: Write in upper and lower case letters and avoid short, blunt-mail messages.
- Assume e-mail is not confidential: If your message is meant to be private, send it another way.
- Check for accuracy: Use correct grammar, spelling and punctuation.
- Follow up: If you fail to receive a timely response, remember to follow up. Your recipient may never have received your message.
- Check your e-mail frequently: Discipline yourself to read and respond to e-mail regularly.

CHAPTER 5

WHAT ARE NEWSGROUPS AND MAILING LISTS?

CHAPTER 5

WHAT ARE NEWSGROUPS AND MAILING LISTS?

WHAT ARE NEWSGROUPS?

Newsgroups are electronic forums for discussing issues, expressing opinions and sharing information. Also known as discussion groups or network news, this free medium draws people from all over the world to discuss over 20,000 very specific topics. USENET is the name of the messaging system used by newsgroups, as well as a term denoting the overall newsgroup community.

Newsgroup discussions are organized by topics. Examples of human resource topics covered include employment, careers, benefits, compensation, and workplace issues. A topic is posted to the group in an article. Some groups are moderated, meaning that a group administrator reads and edits messages before posting them to the group. You can view the articles in a newsgroup without subscribing to the group.

Do not jump into a newsgroup and start making inappropriate statements. Get a sense of the discussion underway before entering the conversation. Be sure to read the FAQ (Frequently Asked Questions) for a newsgroup, if one is available, before posting an article to the group. FAQ's are documents that provide answers to frequently asked questions about the newsgroup.

HOW IS USENET ORGANIZED?

The Seven Standard USENET Group Categories

There are several categories (called hierarchies) of USENET groups that are distributed worldwide. Some groups are subsets of other groups, may only be distributed within a geographic area, and may not operate under the seven standard hierarchies. Access to these alternative hierarchies depends largely on which newsgroups your Internet Service Provider decides to carry as part of their service.

comp

This hierarchy covers newsgroups for computer professionals and computer enthusiasts. Hundreds of groups provide readers with a vast array of knowledge on every aspect of computer hardware and software.

news

This hierarchy covers USENET itself, focusing on discussions about USENET network administration and newsgroups as a topic. By accessing news lists, you can obtain information about the top newsgroups on USENET by topic.

rec

This hierarchy is for discussion on recreational topics, including hobbies, crafts, the arts, and sports. This is not a newsgroup category with information of value to most human resource professionals.

sci

These newsgroups are typically concerned with practical knowledge related to research or applications of science,

What Are Newsgroups And Mailing Lists? 67

including medicine, psychology and other areas of interest to human resource managers.

soc

This hierarchy is concerned with social sciences and social issues, including depression and feminism.

talk

This hierarchy covers controversial issues and is a no-holds-barred forum for debate among those interested in specific topics. Talk newsgroups cover lifestyles (such as gay issues and homophobia), current issues (like drug testing), other cultures (of special interest to human resource managers in multinational companies and those dealing with diversity issues), politics and ethics.

misc

This hierarchy covers anything that isn't easily covered in the above groups, or combines two related topics under one newsgroup. This area includes many business topics and also serves as the USENET marketplace, where users can also find items—particularly computer equipment—for sale.

Alternative Newsgroups

Alternative newsgroups contain a great deal of information of interest to human resources personnel.

alt

The alternative newsgroup hierarchy (alt) contains discussion groups on a wide variety of subjects. The alternative category contains probably the largest group of discussion forums, numbering in the thousands and growing daily.

biz

The biz hierarchy is devoted to business and information about businesses. It includes a breakdown of certain industries, such as computer, medical service, or food service. These sites will include information about a specific company (example: **biz.ibm**), including press releases, their latest financial information (whether the company is publicly traded on stock markets), and even the profiles of executives. Products and services are also covered, including new features and purchase locations.

SELECTING NEWSREADER SOFTWARE

Newsreader Software Options

Newsreader software and access to newsgroups is usually included in Internet access providers' subscription service. The newsreader software allows users to view a listing of available groups, view and respond to articles that have been posted, post articles to the group, and subscribe to newsgroups. These TCP/IP newsreaders use the Network News Transfer Protocol (NNTP). Different newsreaders, such as Netscape, Internet News, Free Agent, WinVN, Newswatcher, and Trumpet, display information in a variety of ways.

Two programs stand out from the crowd.

NETSCAPE

Netscape features a very good newsreader program that is capable of handling binary files. If a message includes an attachment, such as a graphics file, you can view the image in the newsreader window without having to save the file to your hard disk.

MICROSOFT INTERNET NEWS

Microsoft's newsreader program, Internet News, includes an options dialog box (select Next, Options), which enables users to configure Internet News and customize it to their specifications. You can, for example, have Internet News spell-check your articles before posting them, as well as specify how often the news server is checked to see if any new articles have been posted to newsgroups you subscribe to. You can download a free copy of Internet News from *http://www.microsoft.com*.

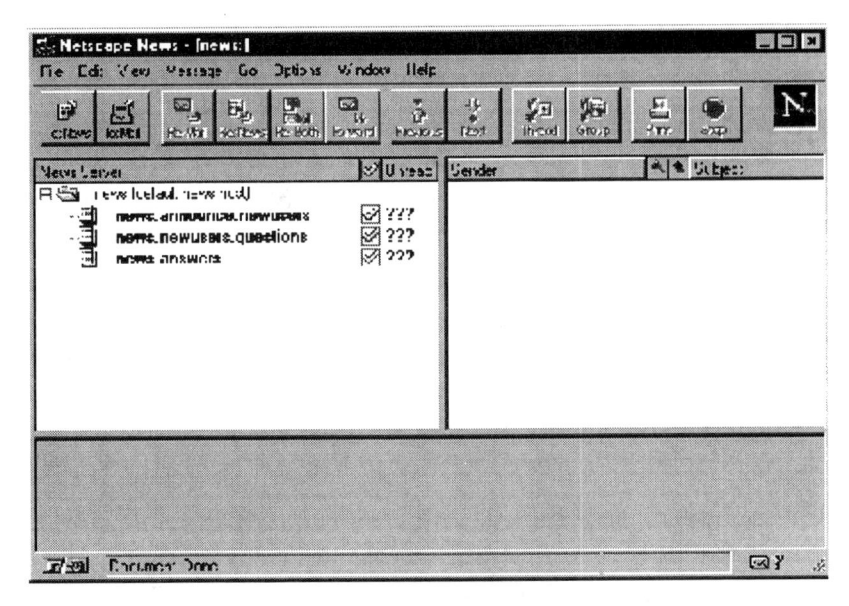

HOW DO I SEARCH HUMAN RESOURCE NEWSGROUPS?

When you're looking for information on a specific subject and you don't know what newsgroup it is in, you can use a USENET searching tool to sort through the maze and pull out just the information you need. One such tool is called DejaNews (*http://www.dejanews.com*). Another is SIFT, the Stanford Information Filtering Tool (*http://sift.stanford.edu*).

WHAT IS A MAILING LIST?

Mailing lists were created by people who wanted an easy, reliable way for a group of people with common interests to communicate by e-mail. Also called listservs, mailing lists cover thousands of topics and interests, allowing people all over the world to efficiently and inexpensively exchange information and messages simultaneously. Their continued growth is limited only by the initiative and imagination of the people who create them.

E-mail messages for a particular mailing list are sent to the administrator (either human or automated), and then in turn delivered by e-mail to those who have subscribed to the mailing list. These messages are delivered to your e-mail box like any other e-mail message.

Each mailing list has two addresses. One address receives messages for the entire group and the other address is for administrative purposes. When you subscribe to a mail list, make sure you send your request to the administrative address.

In a way, subscribing to a mailing list is similar to subscribing to a hardcopy magazine like *HR Today* and relying on receiving a new copy each week, except that mailing list delivery schedules vary from list to list.

Once subscribed, you will start receiving copies of all e-mail messages posted to that particular mailing list. You can just be a 'lurker' (reader) of those messages, or you can choose to participate by responding publicly to the entire mailing list or privately to just one of the list subscribers.

Moderated Mailing Lists

Some mailing lists are moderated. In a moderated mailing list, each message is first read by a volunteer who decides if the message is appropriate for the group. If the message meets the guidelines for the group, it is sent to every person on the list.

A moderated mailing list keeps discussions on-topic and removes messages that discuss the same ideas. In an unmoderated mailing list, all messages are automatically sent to everyone in the group.

Digests

If you receive a lot of messages from a mailing list, check if the list is available as a digest. This groups individual messages together and sends them to you as one message.

Finding Lists

For a list of available mailing lists, visit the Website **http://www.neosoft.com/internet/paml** or go the

news.answers newsgroup and look at the messages with the subject Public Accessible Mailing Lists.

HOW TO SUBSCRIBE TO A MAILING LIST

Just as you would subscribe to a magazine, you must subscribe to a mailing list to join the discussion group. You can unsubscribe from a mailing list at any time. When you subscribe to a mailing list, make sure you frequently check your mailbox. You can receive dozens of messages in a short time.

To subscribe to a mailing list, you first need to find out whether you are sending your request to a software program or a human being. This is very important because knowing whether a list that has a human moderator or is controlled by software determines how you request a subscription. You can usually tell by the mail-to address. If the address includes ***listserve@***, for example, the list is handled by a software program. If the address features the word *request*, it is a toss up as to whether there is a human being or software at the other end.

Subscribe

To join a manually maintained mailing list, simply send an e-mail message to the administrative address. When you subscribe to a mailing list, you will usually receive a "Welcome" message with information that you have been added to the list. Within a few days, you will start receiving messages from the mailing list.

To join an automated list, send a message with the words ***Subscribe listname firstname lastname***. Leave the subject field blank. For example, individuals interested in discussions of training and development for human resources professionals can subscribe to the Training and Development List (TRDEV-L) at ***listserve@psum.psu.edu***. Your message should read ***subscribe trdev-l firstname lastname***. To send a message to the entire list, address your message to ***trdev-l@psuvm.psu.edu***.

Unsubscribe

When you go on vacation, make sure you unsubscribe from all your mailing lists. This will prevent your mailbox from overflowing with messages. To leave a manually maintained mailing list, you simply send an e-mail message to the administrative address. To unsubscribe from an automated list, send a message with the words **unsubcribe mail-list-name**.

MAILING LIST ETIQUETTE

Read the messages in a mailing list for a week before submitting your first message. This is a good way to learn how people in a mailing list communicate and prevents you from submitting information already posted.

You can reply to a message to answer a question or supply additional information. When you send a reply, make sure you include part of the original message. This is called quoting. Quoting helps readers identify which message you are referring to.

If your reply would not be of interest to others in a mailing list or you want to send a private response, send an e-mail message rather than responding to the entire list. Reply to a message only when you have something important to say, not just to agree with another posting.

Mailing lists are a good way to keep informed about a variety of subjects. But be careful not to overload your mailbox. If you subscribe to many different mailing lists, you will receive large amounts of e-mail. It is not impossible to receive several hundred messages in a single day, but it might be impossible to read them all.

HOW CAN I CHAT ONLINE?

What is IRC?

If e-mail is like sending a letter, Internet chat is like conducting a telephone conversation. It is an instantaneous exchange of e-mail messages while both sender and recipient are online.

There are several methods of talking with your associates. Depending on your computer equipment, communications access, and personal preferences, you can choose from a growing variety of Internet chat applications. Two popular ways to conduct a text-based conversation are Internet Relay Chat (IRC) and Netscape Chat.

The IRC system is composed of many interconnected servers all over the world. To join an IRC chat, you must first access an IRC server. If you connect to the Internet through a provider who offers IRC services, simply type *irc* at the command line in a TELNET client window, or download and install one of the many available IRC client programs. Once you connect to an IRC server, select a nickname for yourself and list the available channels. You can join one or more channels or create your own.

IRC also allows you to send and receive private messages and transfer files. Once you are familiar with using IRC, you can operate a secret or private channel that allows only certain users to join. For more information on IRC, including where to find IRC clients and basic IRC commands, go to *http://www.kei-.com/irc.html* and read the IRC FAQ.

Netscape Chat is similar to IRC, but is uses the Netscape Chat client/server technology. To use Netscape Chat, first visit the Netscape Home Page at *http://www.netscape.com/* to download and install the client software. When you log on to a Netscape Chat server, select a nickname and join or create a channel as you would in IRC. As an additional feature, Netscape Chat interfaces with the Netscape Web browser, allowing you to immediately post URLs for others to browse while you continue to chat with them.

MULTIMEDIA CHATTING

If you want to try a multimedia approach to chatting over the Internet, check out WorldsChat at *http://www.worlds-.net/products/wchat/index.html*. This technology allows you to travel around in a three-dimensional virtual space, listen to sounds and music, and bump into other folks and initiate spontaneous conversations.

Once you get used to navigating in WorldsChat, you can meet your friends in the various WorldsChat rooms to participate in a virtual party.

You can also use voice technology that turns your Internet connection into a telephone device. To learn more about voice interaction over the Internet, go to **http://www.north-coast.com/savetz/voice-faq.html** to read the FAQ "How can I use the Internet as a telephone?"

There are many more chat products and services available, including Web-based chat programs. Go to **http://www.yahoo.com/Computers_and_Internet/Internet/Chatting/Products/** to peruse a list of such products.

CHAPTER 6

A DIRECTORY OF HUMAN RESOURCES NEWSGROUPS AND MAILING LISTS

CHAPTER 6
A DIRECTORY OF HUMAN RESOURCES NEWSGROUPS AND MAILING LISTS

HUMAN RESOURCES NEWSGROUPS

ALT.BUSINESS.INSURANCE

Discussion of insurance issues.

ALT.EDUCATION-DISABLED

Discussion of education for people with physical and mental disabilities.

ALT.MANUFACTURING.MISC

Discussion of manufacturing industry issues.

ALT.SEXUAL.ABUSE.RECOVERY

　　Discussion of issues facing victims of sexual abuse.

ALT.SOCIETY.LABOR-UNIONS

　　Discussion of labor union issues.

ALT.SUPPORT

　　Discussion of options for dealing with emotional issues.

ALT.SUPPORT.NON-SMOKERS

　　Discussion of second-hand smoke issues.

BIZ.GENERAL

　　Discussion related to business operations.

BIZ.JOBS.OFFERED

　　Position announcements.

BIZ.LISTSERV.ADA.LAW

　　Discussion about the American with Disabilities Act.

BIZ.LISTSERV.QUALITY

　　Total Quality Management in manufacturing and service industries.

CLARI.BIZ.INDUSTRY.SERVICES

　　Discussion of consulting services.

CLARI.NEWS.SMOKING

　　Smoking and tobacco issues.

CLARI.NEWS.USA.LAW

　　Discussion of legal news and lawsuits.

CLARI.NEWS.WOMEN

　　Discussion of womens issues, including harrassment and sexual discrimination.

MISC.BUSINESS.CONSULTING

Discussion of all aspects of consulting.

MISC. BUSINESS.RECORDS-MANGEMENT

Discussion of all aspects of professional records management.

MISC.INDUSTRY.QUALITY

Discussion of quality standards and related issues.

MISC.JOBS.CONTRACT

Discussion of contract labor issues.

MISC.JOBS.MISC

For discussions about employment, workplace issues, and careers.

MISC.LEGAL.MODERATED

Discussion of all aspects of law.

MISC.TAXES

Discussion of tax laws and related issues.

SOC.ORG.NONPROFIT

Discussion of nonprofit organization issues.

HUMAN RESOURCES MAILING LISTS

ADA-LAW

For discussion of legal aspects of the Americans with Disabilities Act.

Contact: **LISTSERV@NDSUVML.BITNET**

ADDICT-L

For a discussion concerning addictions, awareness, research, education and recovery.

Contact: **LISTSERVE@KENTVM.KENT.EDU**

AFFAM-L
>For discussion of affirmative action issues.

Contact: **LISTSERV@CMSA.BERKELEY.EDU**

AWD
>For a discussion of the American with Disabilities Act.

Contact: **MAJORDOMO@COUNTERPOINT.COM**

BENEFITS-L
>For discussion of employee benefits.

Contact: **LSITSERV@FRANK@MTSU.EDU**

BUSHEA
>Health-related information on business and industry.

Contact: **LISTSERV%IUCVMB.BITNET@LISTSERV.NET**

CARDEVNET
>For discussion of career development topics.

Contact: **CARDEVNET-REQUEST@WORLD.STD.COM**

CAREERNET
>For discussion of career research and management issues.

Contact: **LISTPROC@CREDIT.ERIN.UTORONTO.CA**

CHANGE
>For a discussion on professional change in organizations.

Contact: **MAJORDOMO@MINDSPRING.COM**

DISPUTE-RES
>An Alternative Dispute Resolution discussion group.

Contact: **LISTSERV@LISTSERV.LAW.CORNELL.EDU**

DIVERSITY-FORUM

For discussion of diversity issues.

Contact: **MAJORDOMO@IGE.APE.ORG**

EAP

For discussion of employee assistance counseling issues.

Contact: **LISTPROC@PGE.COM**

FLEXWORK

For discussion on flexible work hours.

Contact: **LISTSERV@PSUHMC.HMC.PSU.EDU**

H-LABOR

For discussion of labor history.

Contact: **LISTSERV@UICVM.UIC.EDU**

HRD-L

For discussion of all human resources topics.

Contact: **MAJORDOMO@CYBERTOUCH.COM**

HRIS-L

For discussion of MIS issues in human resources.

Contact: **MAJORDOMO@CYBERTOUCH.COM**

HRNET

For discussion of general human resources information.

Contact: **LISTSERV@CORNELL.EDU**

HR-OD-L

For discussion of human resources and organizational development.

Contact: **LISTSERV@KSUVM.KSU.EDU**

IERN-L

For discussion of industrial relations and human resource management.

Contact: **LISTSERV@UBE.UBALT.EDU**

IOOB-L

For discussion of industrial psychology topics.

Contact: **LISTSERV@UGA.CC.EGA.EDU**

IPMAAC-LIST

Discussion list of the International Personnel Management Association's Assessment Council.

Contact: **MAJORDOMO@LISTS.BEST.COM**

IRRA

A discussion group of the Industrial Relations Research Association.

Contact: **LISTSERV@RELAY.DOIT.WISC.EDU**

JOBANALYSIS

For discussion of job analysis techniques.

Contact: **LISTSERV@VT.EDU**

JOBPLACE

For a discussion of job search techniques.

Contact: **LISTSERV@UKCC.UKY.EDU**

JOBPLACE

For a discussion of self-directed job search techniques and job placement.

Contact: **LISTSERV@NEWS.JOBWEB.ORG**

JOB-TECH

Discussions on technology and employment.

Contact: **LISTSERV@LISTSERV.VT.EDU**

LABNEWS
For a discussion on news of labor unions and workplace organizing.

Contact: **LISTSERV@CMSA.BERKELEY.EDU**

LABOR-L
A discussion group for the North American labor movement.

Contact: **LISTSERV@VM1.YORKU.CA**

MGTDEV-L
Management and executive development topics.

Contact: **LISTSERV@MIAMIU.MUOHIO.EDU**

NWAC-L
For discussion of the changing nature of work.

Contact: **LISTSERV@PSUVM.PSU.EDU**

ODCNET-L
For discussion of organizational development issues.

Contact: **LISTSERV@PSUVM.PSU.EDU**

ODNET
A discussion group of the National Organizational Development Network.

Contact: **MAJORDOMO@LISTS.TMN.COM**

PAYHR-L
For discussion of human resources and payroll issues.

Contact: **LISTSERV@VM1.UCC.OKSTATE.EDU**

PRIR-L
For discussion of industrial relations in Australia and New Zealand.

Contact: **LISTPROC@LIST.WAIKATO.AC.NZ**

SOREHAND

For discussion of typing-related injuries.

Contact: **LISTSERV@UCSFVM.UCSF.EDU**

TESLSB-L

For a discussion on jobs and employment issues.

Contact: **LISTSERV@CUNYUM.CUNY.EDU**

TRDEV-L

For a discussion on training and development topics.

Contact: **LISTSERV@PSUVM.PSU.EDU**

UNION-D

A European trade union discussion group.

Contact: **LISTSERV@WOLFNET.COM**

UNITE

A labor network discussion group.

Contact: **FTPSERVER@COUGAR.COM**

CHAPTER 7

WHAT ABOUT THE WORLD WIDE WEB?

CHAPTER 7

WHAT ABOUT THE WORLD WIDE WEB?

"WHAT CAN THE WEB DO FOR ME?"

You can use WWW services to:
- Search for, retrieve, and read literally billions of files stored on computers throughout the world.
- Search for and retrieve shareware, freeware, and commercial software.
- Search databases of organizations, individuals, and government sources for files on thousands of topics.
- Browse through public and private information sources.
- Search library catalogs at many public, university, and research libraries.
- Search for and order magazine articles.
- Set up a web page for your company and its products.

WHAT IS THE WORLD WIDE WEB (WWW)?

It's not the Internet, although it uses the Internet (and other networks) as a communication medium. The World Wide Web refers to the body of information (huge collections of documents, called Web pages) available through millions of networked computers, while the Internet refers to the physical side of the global network—the countless cables, hardware, and computers that make the Web possible.

The Web has two significant characteristics that differentiate it from other Internet information systems—interactive multimedia and hyperlinks. Interactive multimedia refers to the fact that the Web lets you access a variety of media and resources—documents, graphics, photographs, audio and video— and bring them directly to your computer, monitor and/or stereo speakers.

Hyperlinks

Hyperlinks are electronic pointers that allow you jump from one Web resource to another by simply clicking on them with your computer mouse. Hyperlinks can be embedded in

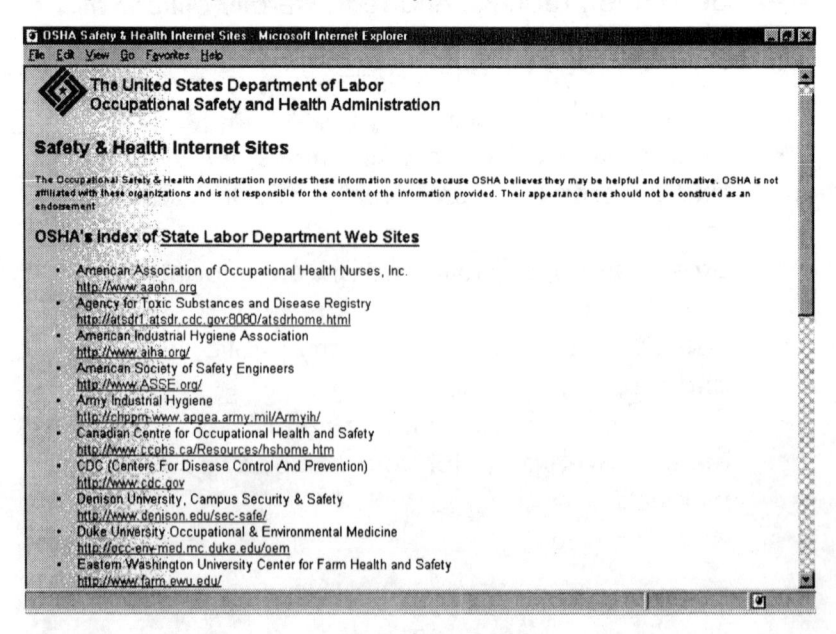

What About The World Wide Web? 89

the text or graphics of a Web page. They are generally underlined and appear in a different color. In addition, your mouse cursor will change into a "hand" when it is positioned on a hyperlink.

HOW DOES THE WEB WORK?

The Web works using the client-server model. A Web server is a program running continuously on a computer whose sole purpose is to "serve" files to other computers that ask for them. A Web client is a program (a browser, like Netscape or Microsoft Internet Explorer) that interfaces with the user (usually through hypertext pages) and request documents from the server as the user asks for them. The principal language that Web clients and servers use to communicate with each other is called the Hypertext Transport Protocol (HTTP).

The standard language used on the Web for creating and recognizing hypermedia documents is called Hypertext Markup Language (HTML). Web documents written in HTML can be identified by their ".html" suffix.

World Wide Web Addresses

HTML uses addresses that are called Universal Resource Locators (URLs) to represent hyperlinks and links to network services within documents. Each URL begins with the protocol used to access the link, typically HTTP (Hypertext Transport Protocol) or FTP (File Transfer Protocol).

The second part of the URL (after the //) is the computer address, a directory path for the computer, followed by the domain type, which describes the type of entity responsible for the site (business, government, etc.), and a file name (.html or .htm extensions mean the file contains links to other web pages).

The domain type in a Web address indifies the type of entity behind the Web site. Listed below are the definitions associated with the most common domain type abbreviations.

com   commercial business (companies)
edu   education (colleges, universities, schools)

gov government (federal, state, or local, non-military)
mil US military
net network organizations
org miscellaneous organizations

Other domain types include abbreviations for country names (*ca* stands for Canada, *au* is Australia's abbreviation, *at* represents Austria, etc.)

What is a Web Page?

A Web page is the basic building block of the World Wide Web. A Web page can contain information in a variety of media, including sophisticated graphics, audio and video. A Web site can consist of just one page or up to one hundred pages.

If a Web page has a large photograph, it may take 10 minutes to load. It is wise to use small graphics, so that users can access pages in a reasonable amount of time.

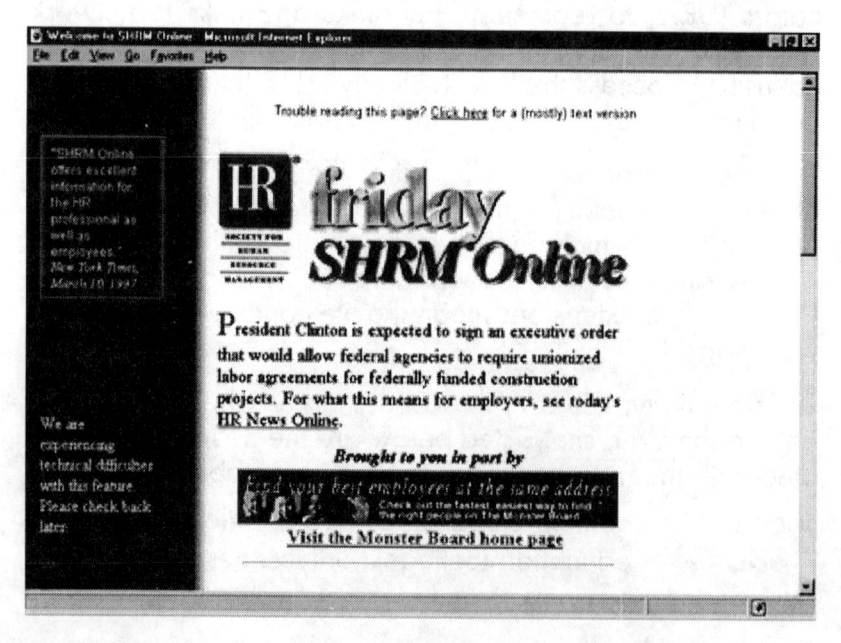

While most Web pages are accessible with all browsers, some pages can only be viewed with a specific browser. If your company is considering creating a Web page, remember to look at it with as many Web browsers as possible. Many people use Netscape, but Prodigy, CompuServe, and AOL have millions of users as well. So take a look at your Web pages to make sure they're at least legible regardless of which browser users are using.

Should You Have a Web Site?

The Web offers companies a new way to communicate with employers and customers, projecting an attractive appearance while simultaneously selling their services or goods. Companies can put their catalogs on the Web, and even let customers place an order instantly. Before long, any company without a Web site will be at a considerable disadvantage.

Your Web site will be accessible to millions of people. They will draw conclusions about your organization based on your site. Your site should reflect your organization's image and must be regularly updated.

Think about users needs, as well as your own goals, when you plan your Web site. If you provide valuable information, users will respond to your message, even if it's an advertisement.

CHAPTER 8

HOW CAN I GET WHAT I WANT FROM THE INTERNET?

CHAPTER 8
HOW CAN I GET WHAT I WANT FROM THE INTERNET?

NET TOOLS

A variety of different software tools are used to retrieve information from Internet and World Wide Web resources. Some predate the Web, like TELNET and Gopher, while Web search engines are recent inventions. But each type of tool serves important information gathering needs.

TELNET

TELNET is one of the oldest protocols and applications on the Net and still one of the most versatile. TELNET is a Terminal Emulation protocol that permits a computer to log on to another computer system on the Internet as a user. Most often, a text-only menu is presented. If you are accessing the system through an on-line service, a separate window will open, usually showing white text on a black background and a blinking cursor. Don't be alarmed: you will see instructions for logging on, as well as how to exit from the system.

TELNET is not the most glamorous method of getting information, but it is one of the most powerful. And there are some things on the Net reachable only via TELNET. Many library catalogs, for example, are accessible only this way.

GOPHER

While the World Wide Web is certainly the most popular part of the Internet, it has limitations. Because the Net has been around since the 1960's and the Web is a recent innovation, there is an enormous amount of information available on the Internet that does not exist on Web pages.

Welcome to the domain of Gopher. Gopher is an Internet application that catalogs millions of files residing on computers all over the worked and makes them easy to retrieve. How did Gopher get its name? It 'goes-for' information requested by the user by 'tunneling' through the Net. Also, the Gopher program was developed at the University of Minnesota, whose football team is known as the Golden Gophers.

How does Gopher differ from the Web?

Gopher is pure text and there are none of the graphics and icons that dominate the Web. But Gopher quickly proves its power to find and retrieve information. 'Gopherspace'—the sum total of all resources cataloged by all Gopher servers in the world—is composed of millions of documents and files.

It's often possible to find more in-depth information with Gopher than with the Web. Libraries, universities, corporations, and foundations make many of their vast resources available via Gopher—reports, essays, reviews, technical papers, statistics, research studies, doctoral dissertations, newspaper archives, library catalogs, on-line dictionaries, and other files that no one has created a Web page to display.

How does Gopher work?

Each Gopher server does two things: it catalogs the information within its own domain (its home university, for instance), and it talks to other Gopher servers. Communication between these Gopher servers is the key to Gopher—

How Can I Get What I Want From The Internet? 97

the ability to connect to a computer system where the information you're looking for is likely to be found. You don't need to know the name of that other computer or where it is.

Since Gopher presents uniform text menus, you may not even realize you've left one computer for another. Each item on a menu may represent information located on a different computer system, but if you want it, just click on it and Gopher takes you to it.

Almost all Internet access providers give their users access to Gopher. If you use one of the major on-line services, you'll probably find Gopher in the Internet area of your service (America Online even has a gopher mascot to guide its users). If you access the Net via a SLIPP/PPP account with an Internet service provider, your provider will likely provide

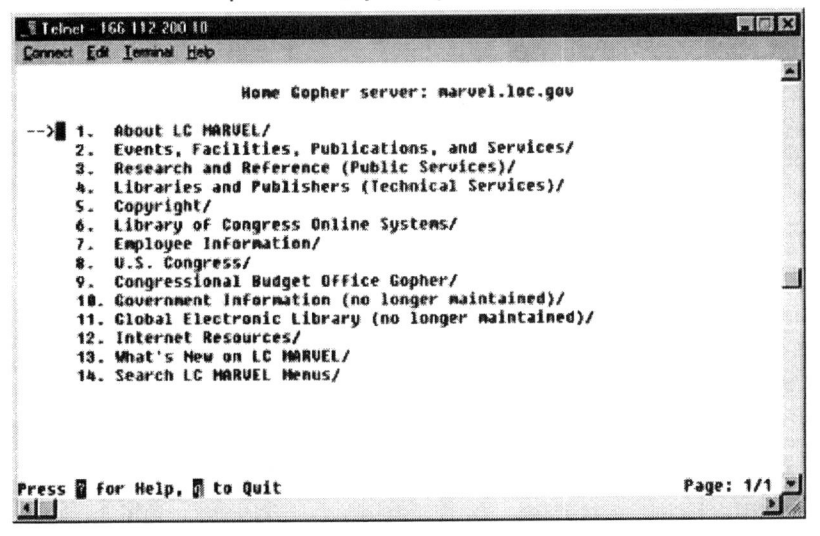

```
Telnet - 166.112.200.10
Connect Edit Terminal Help

                    Home Gopher server: marvel.loc.gov

-->  1. About LC MARVEL/
     2. Events, Facilities, Publications, and Services/
     3. Research and Reference (Public Services)/
     4. Libraries and Publishers (Technical Services)/
     5. Copyright/
     6. Library of Congress Online Systems/
     7. Employee Information/
     8. U.S. Congress/
     9. Congressional Budget Office Gopher/
    10. Government Information (no longer maintained)/
    11. Global Electronic Library (no longer maintained)/
    12. Internet Resources/
    13. What's New on LC MARVEL/
    14. Search LC MARVEL Menus/




Press ? for Help, Q to Quit                                Page: 1/1
```

software for a separate Gopher application to run as part of the startup package. If you're using a text-only account, look for Gopher under 'Applications' on your service's mail screen.

Every Gopher system begins by showing you a basic menu of items from which to choose. It will 'fetch' information from the Net and present it in the form of menus (numbered lists of items from which to choose). The menus that Gopher presents are nested (the item you choose from the first list will often lead to other lists, each of the lists becoming more specific as you approach the target). You use Gopher's menus to 'tunnel down' to the information you seek, which may be a text file, a graphic, or even a sound file.

Advanced functions

"Other Gopher Information Servers" is your ticket to the wider world of Gopherspace. Click on this item and you'll be presented with another list, which will include an item labeled "All the Gopher Servers in the World."

This will present a long list of Gopher servers arranged by continent and county. If you're looking for information on safety, for example, you'll find it with just three mouse clicks.

Another item will be labeled "Gopher Jewels." Click on this and you'll be met with a handy menu of major categories of information, such as law and medicine. Each item will take you deeper into lists devoted to that particular subject. Lastly, Gopher programs usually give you a way to create 'bookmarks' that will help you to develop a list of favorite places to visit in Gopherspace.

Even if you never expect to use Gopher, you'll probably encounter it in your travels on the Web. Most Web browsers can view Gopher menus, and it's becoming common to find links between Web sites and Gopher.

VERONICA

Gopher can easily go up and down the tunnels you dig, but it can't go 'across' to the middle of another tunnel. If you're headed down a dead end during a search, you'll have to go back at least a few menus before you can restart your search. It's also impossible to tell whether what you want is in a certain place until you get there.

Both of these problems are solved by a Gopherspace search engine called Veronica. Veronica stands for Very Easy Rodents-Oriented Net-wide Index to Computerized Archives. Veronica finds resources by searching for specific words in document titles. It does not do a full-text search of the contents of documents. You will usually see two types of Veronica searches: "Search Gopherspace by title words"

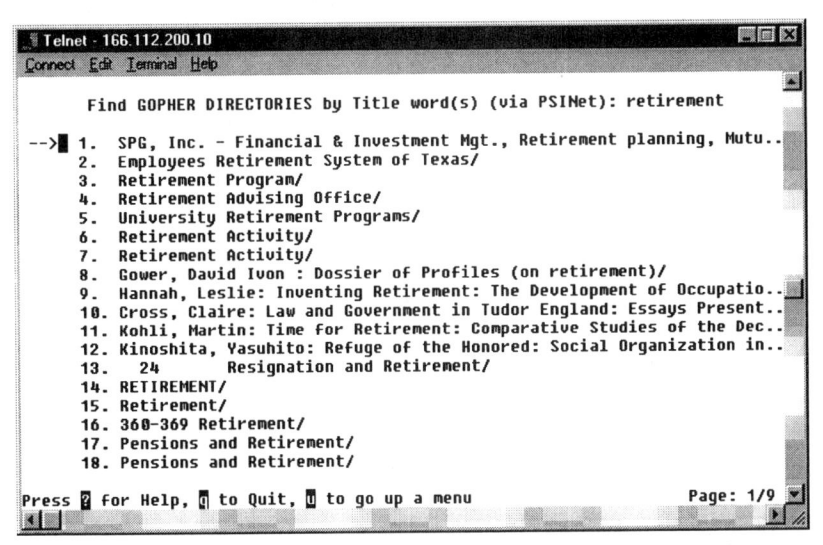

```
 Telnet - 166.112.200.10
 Connect  Edit  Terminal  Help

         Find GOPHER DIRECTORIES by Title word(s) (via PSINet): retirement
 -->  1.  SPG, Inc. - Financial & Investment Mgt., Retirement planning, Mutu..
      2.  Employees Retirement System of Texas/
      3.  Retirement Program/
      4.  Retirement Advising Office/
      5.  University Retirement Programs/
      6.  Retirement Activity/
      7.  Retirement Activity/
      8.  Gower, David Ivon : Dossier of Profiles (on retirement)/
      9.  Hannah, Leslie: Inventing Retirement: The Development of Occupatio..
     10.  Cross, Claire: Law and Government in Tudor England: Essays Present..
     11.  Kohli, Martin: Time for Retirement: Comparative Studies of the Dec..
     12.  Kinoshita, Yasuhito: Refuge of the Honored: Social Organization in..
     13.     24       Resignation and Retirement/
     14.  RETIREMENT/
     15.  Retirement/
     16.  360-369 Retirement/
     17.  Pensions and Retirement/
     18.  Pensions and Retirement/

 Press ? for Help, q to Quit, u to go up a menu           Page: 1/9
```

and "Search Gopher directories by title words." The former searches everything in Gopherspace, menu names as well as the titles of documents themselves. The resources may be any type of data, including ASCII text, gopher directories, images, and binary files.

"Search Gopher directories" is a more limited search, which will find only Gopher menu items whose titles contain your keywords. This type of search can be useful to find only major holdings of information related to your subject. After Veronica finds the relevant Gopher directories, you can open any of them to see the contents in detail.

"Search Gopherspace with Veronica" appears on most Gopher menus. You can access Veronica by pointing your Gopher client or Web browser to **gopher:// veronica.scs.unr.edu/11/veronica**. From here, you will see a list of several Veronica server sites. Some servers may be more up-to-date than others, so there will be some difference in the results. Be sure to read the "How to Compose Veronica Queries" file that includes a number of ways to fine-tune your Veronica searches, making them faster and more productive.

ARCHIE

Remember Archie comic books? Veronica was one of Archie's girlfriends, and before there was a Veronica (the search program), there was Archie (short for 'archiver'), a program that locates File Transfer Protocol (FTP) files, usually computer programs, on the Internet. In an Archie search, you must know at least part of the name of the file you are looking for. Archie will not search for general topics or keywords.

Like Gopher and WAIS searches, Archie searches can be run either from a program on your own computer (if you have a SLIP/PPP account) or an on-line service. Archie searches can be most productive when you're looking for a specific program.

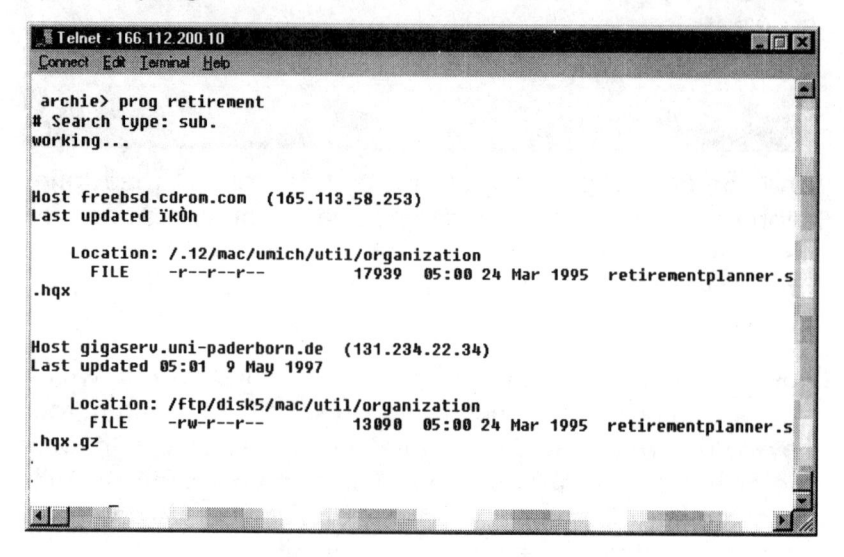

```
Telnet - 166.112.200.10
Connect Edit Terminal Help

archie> prog retirement
# Search type: sub.
working...

Host freebsd.cdrom.com   (165.113.58.253)
Last updated 1k0h

        Location: /.12/mac/umich/util/organization
             FILE    -r--r--r--         17939   05:00 24 Mar 1995   retirementplanner.s
.hqx

Host gigaserv.uni-paderborn.de   (131.234.22.34)
Last updated 05:01  9 May 1997

        Location: /ftp/disk5/mac/util/organization
             FILE    -rw-r--r--         13090   05:00 24 Mar 1995   retirementplanner.s
.hqx.gz
```

You can access Archie via TELNET to a public Archie server, or through e-mail. TELNET to archie.internic.net and log in as archie. Once you are in, type "help" for instructions. Or, to use Archie through electonic mail, send a message to **archie@archie.cs.mcgill.ca** with the word "help" in the message body.

WAIS

One of Gopher's limitations is that while it can uncover (with Veronica) remarkable sources of information, Gopher can only judge a file by its 'cover'. Ask Veronica to find information on safety, for instance, and you'll probably get back a list of a hundred or more links or files, all with the word "safety" in the title. But what Veronica won't find are files that mention safety but don't have the word in their titles. Veronica's weakness in this respect could result in overlooking articles on safety.

WAIS (pronounced ways), which stands for Wide Area Information Server, fills this gap. WAIS is a full-text search engine. Of course, WAIS doesn't really scan entire texts every time you ask a question. It depends on databases of the full texts of hundreds of sources, previously indexed and cross-referenced. WAIS also ranks the information it returns in order of relevance to your query. If it brings back answers that are not precisely what you had in mind, WAIS will go back and search again based on your refined query.

WAIS has its limitations, of course. Its databases are not encyclopedic, and if what you're looking for hasn't been indexed in a WAIS database, WAIS won't find it. On the other hand, WAIS is free and easy to operate, so if you haven't found what you're looking for using other search methods, WAIS is certainly worth a shot. Like Gopher, WAIS programs can run either on a host computer (on an online service, for example) or on your home machine (if you have a SLIP/PPP connection).

FTP

Sooner or later, you're going to want to download something from the Internet. Downloading is the process of copying a file from a remote computer to your computer so that you can read or run it.

Every online service has its own file libraries and download mechanisms, but in the Internet, almost all file transfers are handled by a method called FTP (File Transfer Protocol). FTP is a very powerful and flexible method of transporting and managing files on the Net—not only can you download files to your own computer, but you can also upload files from your 'home' machine onto a remote computer.

As is the case with Gopher, Archie, and other programs described above, you'll be using FTP either through an interface supplied by an online service or through an FTP program running on your computer via a SLIP/PPP connection.

Most SLIP/PPP accounts will include a basic FTP utility as part of the startup package. More sophisticated FTP programs are available as shareware on the Net. Many Web browsers, such as Netscape, can also handle FTP transfers automatically.

The most common use of FTP programs is to copy files from a remote computer (known as an FTP site) by means of a procedure known as Anonymous FTP. In Anonymous FTP, you're actually logging into a remote computer (using the word "anonymous" as your login name and your e-mail address as your password) and copying files to your own system. If you're using FTP through an on-line service, you won't have to worry about a login and password, as the on-line service's system will handle that. If you're using an FTP program on your computer, just select the "anonymous" box in the configuration dialog box.

To transfer files from an FTP site to your computer, you'll need to know both the name of the file you're looking for and the exact directory in which it resides on the host computer. Fortunately, most magazine articles or Internet sites that mention a program or file that you might want to FTP will also give you the information you'll need in a standard address format.

FTP is one of the Internet's core applications. It's definitely worth the time to master it. Besides allowing you to take advantage of the vast software resources available on the Net, FTP can gather some of the best resources on the Net.

Any long text file, will probably be too long to be found on a Web site or in a newsgroup, and may not be available via Gopher or WAIS. In cases like these, a basic familiarity with FTP will not only allow you to access the file, but after downloading it to your computer, it will give you plenty of time to read the file off-line (especially valuable if you're paying timed on-line service charges).

WHAT IS A SEARCH ENGINE?

Search engines are the tools used to 'find needles in the Internet haystack'. With more than 20 million Web pages available, finding what you're looking for on the World Wide Web can be confusing. There are more than 20 search engines from which to choose. Web crawler, Lycos, Yahoo, Alta Vista and Infoseek are some of the most popular.

The search engines function like libraries' card catalogs. They categorize or index information within a Web page or Web site. Search engines are Web pages that allow you to type in a key word, or search term. The search engine then performs a search through its database for Web pages that contain the key word.

For example, if you are interested in finding information on human resources, you would type "human resources" and click on the search button. In a few seconds, a list of sites containing the word human resources would appear (some search engines actually retrieve the sites they find as well). The list will include hypertext links to each site. Simply click the mouse on the link for the site that best matches your interests.

All search engines perform the same basic task but present the information in different ways. Some search engines index by broad categories, while others rank sites based on their own criteria, or list sites based on the number of times the key word is present in the Web page.

CHOOSING A SEARCH ENGINE

Don't let the term 'search engine' scare you. All you have to do is type in the subject you are interested in, click on a button and sit back. Each engine has its own particular strengths and weaknesses, so if at first you don't succeed in finding what you are looking for, try another one.

Alta Vista

One of the newest of the Web search engines, Alta Vista has the largest database of Web pages and USENET newsgroups. It also offers the fastest Web searches available. Best of all, it indexes the entire Web document, so that searching Alta Vista can turn up documents that mention your search words only. To get the best results from AltaVista, you need to learn how to use the service's Advanced Query Options. Still, it is the best way to find that needle-in-a-haystack document. If it's out there, you can bet Alta Vista's database has it.

Alta Vista Services

URL: *http://www.altavista.digital.com*

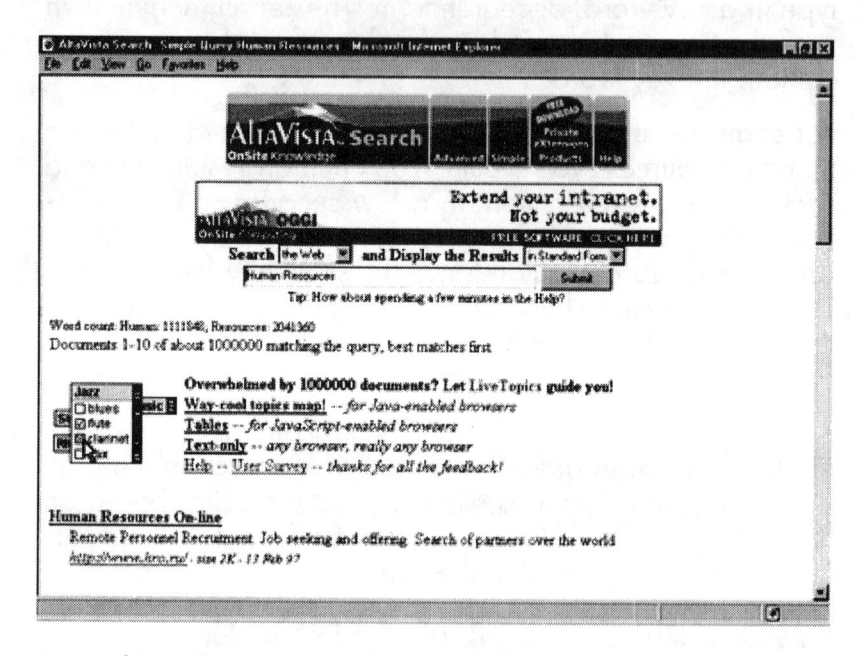

Size of Database: 21 million Web pages, 13,000 USENET newsgroups

Search Options: You can restrict the search to title, URL, host or link. For USENET articles, you can restrict the search to subject, newsgroup, summary, or keywords.

Excite

Excite maintains its currency through the use of "spiders", web robots that search for keywords within web sites. It searches for changes on two million web sites weekly, with tours of the remaining sites of the Web every three weeks. Searches of web sites and newsgroups are aided by the use of "channels" that organize web sites by categories.

Excite Services

URL: *http://www.excite.com*

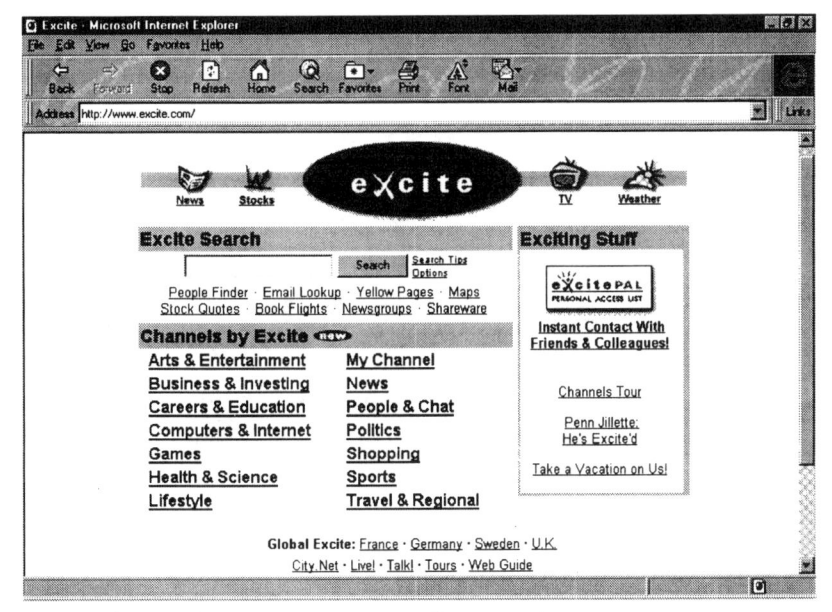

Size of Database: Over 50 million web pages.

Search Options: You can start the search by topic ("channels") and restrict searches to selected web sites or contextually.

Info Seek

One of the Web's most popular search engines (it performs three million searches each day) and by far the most precise on the Web. Its simple searches are designed to let inexperienced users achieve high-precision. Info Seek has a smaller database than some of the other indexes, but it searches much faster. It is often the quickest way to find a Web page.

Info Seek Services

URL: *http://www.infoseek.com*

Size of Database: More than one million Web pages and over 10,000 USENET groups.

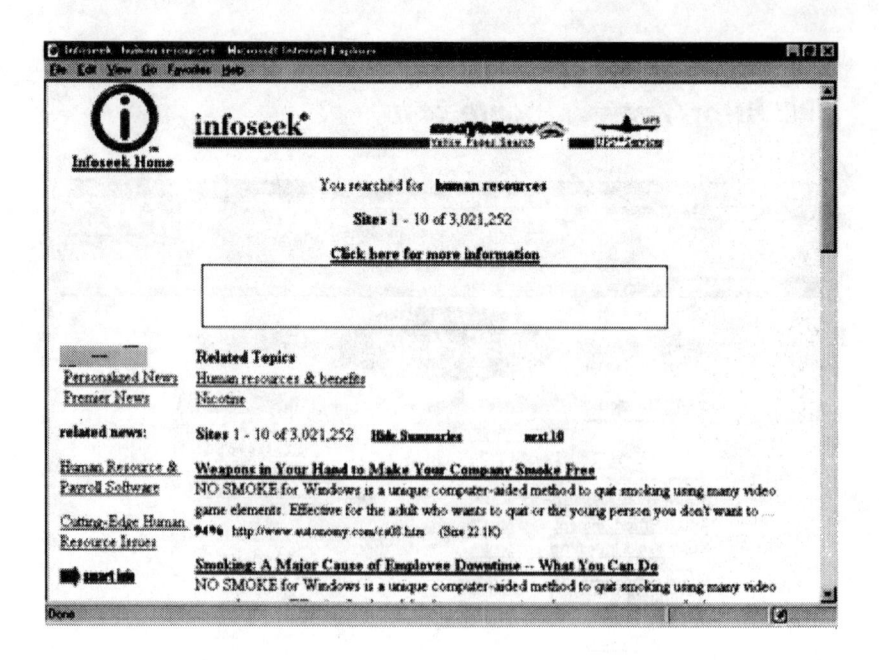

Search Options:
- Keyword Search.
- Newsgroups. You will find more than 10,00 USENET newsgroups.
- USENET FAQs. Frequently Asked Questions for newsgroups.
- Reviewed pages. Only those Web pages that Info Seek has reviewed are searched.

Lycos

Before Alta Vista came along, Lycos was the largest database. It currently indexes more than five million URLs and over two million documents. Lycos is sometimes difficult to access during peak usage times and it does not index entire documents. Instead, it indexes title words, the words found in the first few lines of text, and the most frequently-occurring words in the rest of the document. Lycos searches are fairly low in precision, and may fail to retrieve relevant documents.

Lycos Services

URL: *http://www.lycos.com*

Size of Database: 10.8 million documents

How Can I Get What I Want From The Internet?

Search Options:

- Formless searching. Lycos displays nothing more than a simple text box in which you type the key words for which you are searching.
- Form-based searching. Allows users to use 'and' and 'or' with keywords in the search field and specify output options.

Web Crawler

Web Crawler is an automated indexer that categorizes and indexes every page it comes across. When the search is complete, Web Crawler displays a list of Web pages that contain the word specified. Web Crawler retrieves the entire text of the documents it finds, but you will find that most of the retrieved documents are irrelevant.

Web Crawler Services

URL: *http://www.webcrawler.com*

Size of Database: 1.8 millionWeb pages

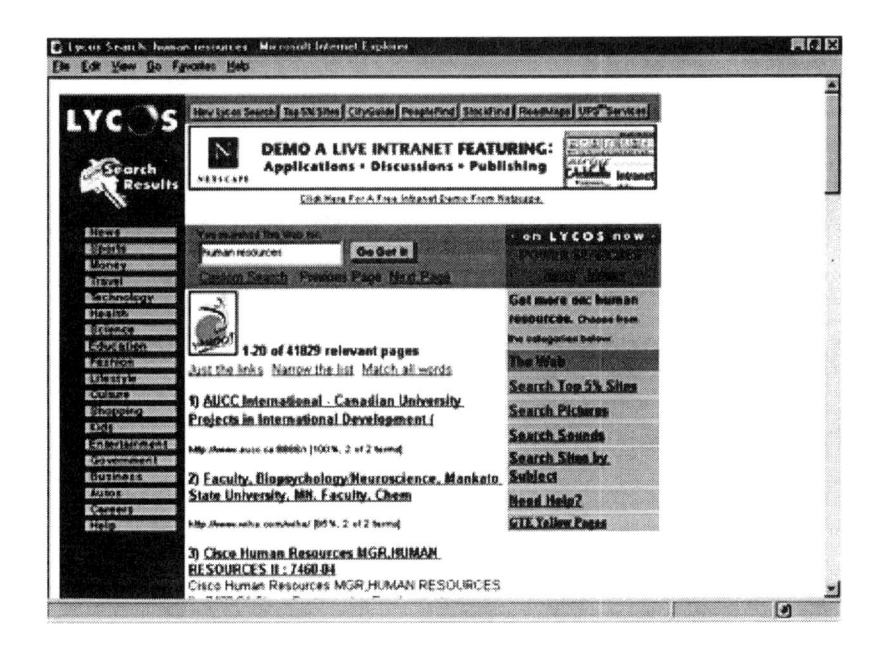

Search Options: Key word search.

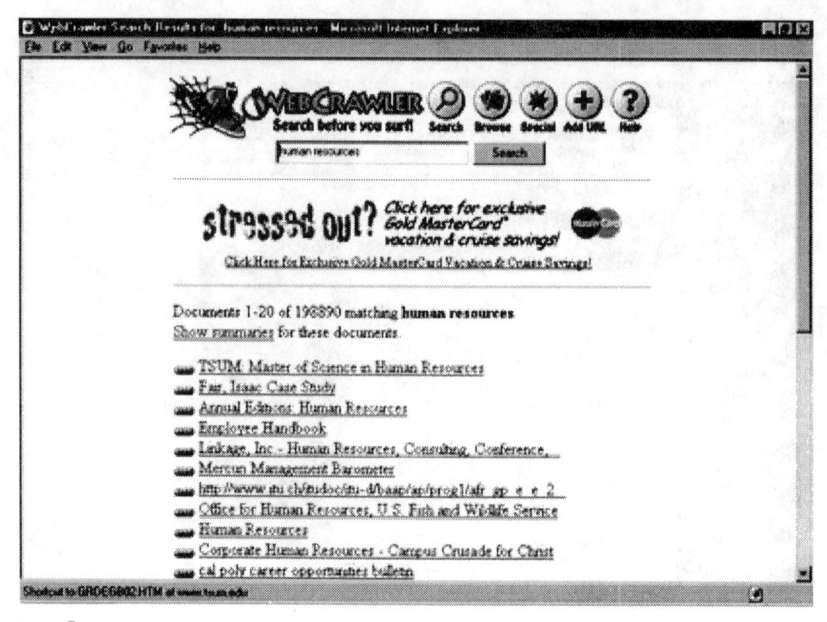

Yahoo

Yahoo's off beat name has made it a big hit among many Web users. Yahoo stands for Yet Another Hierarchically Odiferous Oracle. As search engines, Yahoo is on of the best. It's easy to use, and it's packed with information that

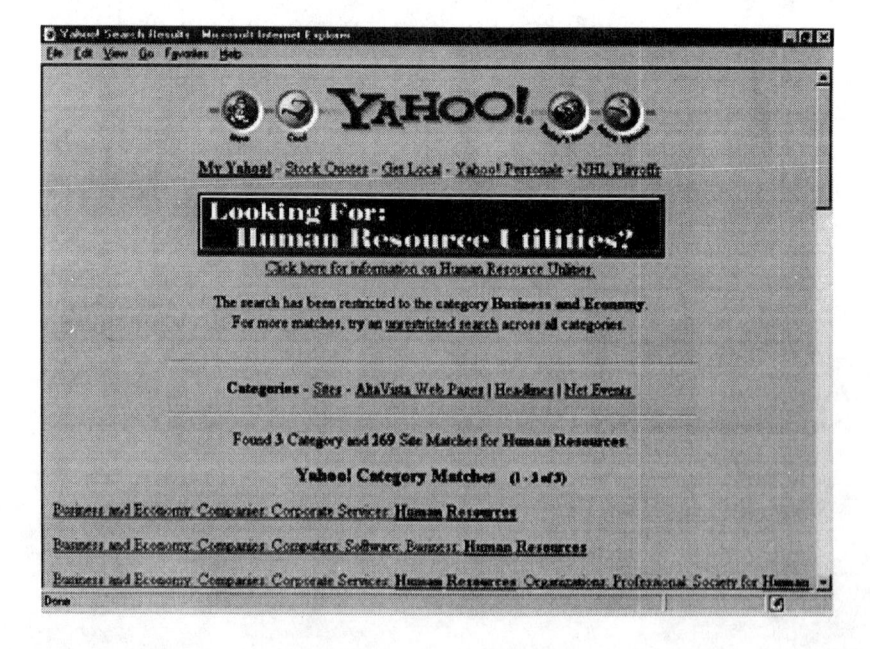

Web users want. Search results are displayed as a list of documents, ranked numerically by relevance. The first few lines of text from the Web page are provided.

Yahoo Services

URL: *http://www.yahoo.com*

Size of Database: 15 million documents

Search Options: Keyword search.

CHAPTER 9

A DIRECTORY OF HUMAN RESOURCES WEB SITES

CHAPTER 9

A DIRECTORY OF HUMAN RESOURCES WEB SITES

Below is a list of Web sites of interest to human resources professionals. This list is not intended to be a complete directory, but is an overview of the types of resources available. Some addresses may have changed since the list was compiled.

ADDICTION

Ameritest

http://www.ameritest.com

This is a nationwide service for workplace drug and alcohol testing.

Hazelden

http://www.hazelden.com

This site, created by a non-profit organization helping people recovering from alcohol and drug addiction, explains the dangers that using controlled substances can pose to employees.

Prevention OnLine

> *http://www.health.org*

This is the world's largest resource for current information on alcohol and other drugs. You can search the National Substance Abuse Web to locate information indexed from 22 different substance prevention and treatment Web sites.

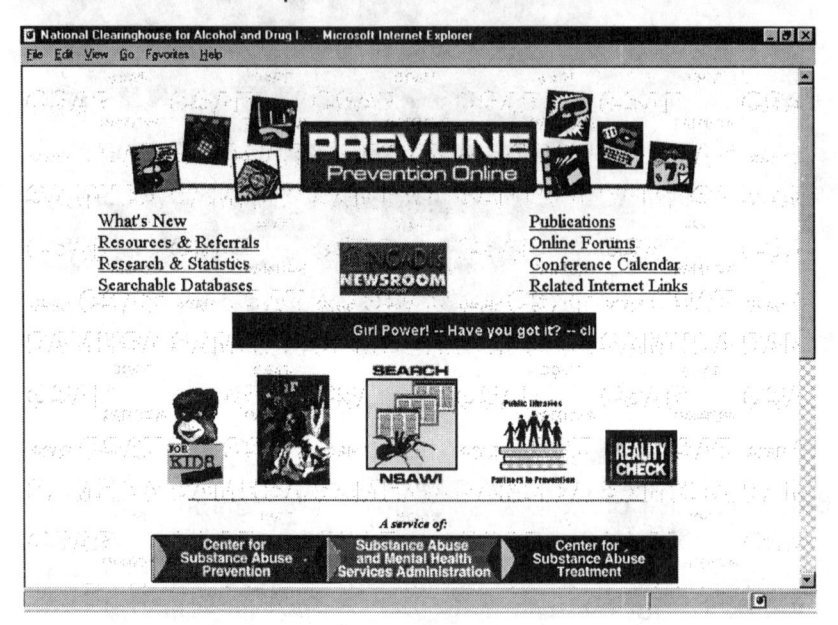

AFFIRMATIVE ACTION

American Association for Affirmative Action

> *http://www.fga.com/aaaa*

Organization supporting affirmative action, equal opportunity and elimination of discrimination, providing news, overviews, and federal and state laws, legislation and regulations.

Berkshire Associates

> *http://www.berkshire-aap.com*

Software program facilitates affirmative action programs, handling statistical reports and data.

Criterion Inc.
http://www.criterioninc.com

Software for managing affirmative action plans, succession and career planning, and training.

Employee Relations Web Picks
http://www.nyper.com

Links are provided to Web sites covering affirmative action, the Americans with Disabilities Act, collective bargaining, and employment law.

Equal Opportunity Publications
http://www.eop.com/ccwd/homepage.html

EOP has a career center for workforce diversity. For over 27 years, it has led the way in affirmative action, diversity recruitment for minorities, women, and people with disabilities by publishing career magazines entitled *Equal Opportunity, Women Engineer, Minority Engineer, Careers and the Disabled*, and *Workforce Diversity*.

PRI Associates
http://www.priassoc.com

State of the art affirmative action planning and skills assessment software solutions.

SER Jobs for Progress National
http://www.sernational.org

This site's special emphasis is on the needs of Hispanics in education, job skill training, employment, and literacy.

Sex Discrimination
http://www.firstfloor.com/catalogs/hr2.htm

A series of articles on sexual discrimination in the workplace, covering comparable worth, dress codes, grooming standards, and pregnancy issues.

ASSESSMENT

Assessment Systems Inc.
http://www.acaonline.org

Information on selecting, assessing, hiring, and developing outstanding employees.

CSBAN
http://www.csban.org/bgt/hr/evalcom.html

Information on workforce evaluation, including the components of an employee evaluation (assessment, written performance appraisals, oral review interviews, etc.)

ASSOCIATIONS

Academy of Management
http://www.aom.pace.edu

Leading professional association for management research and education in the United States explores and tests new management concepts.

American Compensation Association
http://www.ahrm.org/aca/aca.htm

The ACA is a not-for-profit association with over 20,000 members who are engaged in the design, implementation and management of employee compensation and benefits programs in their respective organizations.

American Arbitration Association of Dispute Resolution Services
http://www.adr.org

Web site focuses on commercial, corporate, insurance, labor, and employment with rules and procedures, topics of interest, guides, arbitration, ethics and standards, current articles, and press releases on each.

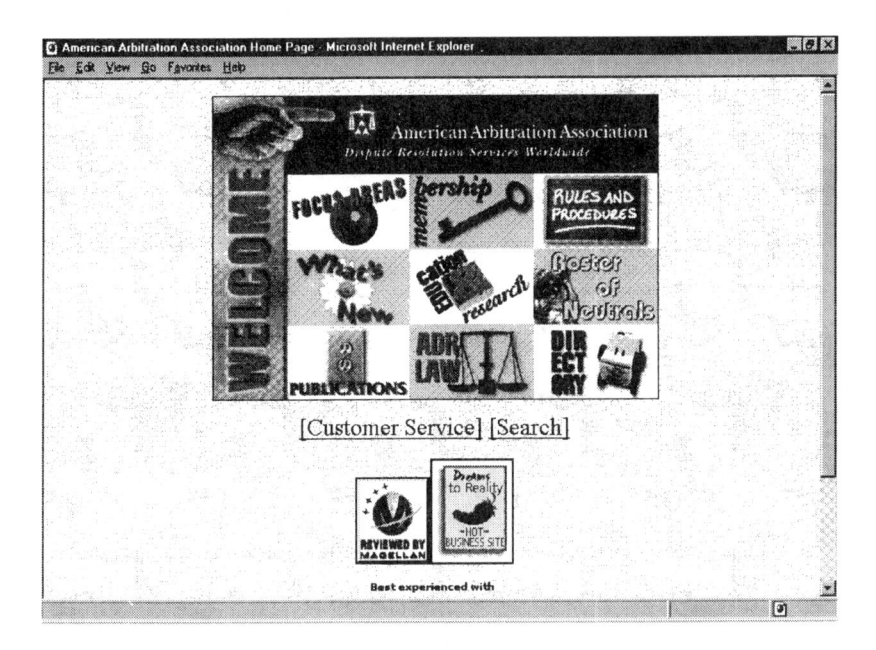

American Association for Affirmative Action

http://www.fga.com/aaaa

Organization supporting affirmative action, equal opportunity and elimination of discrimination, providing news, overviews, and federal and state laws, legislation and regulations.

American Association of Colleges and Employers (NACE)

http://www.jobweb.org

Helps thousands of college career services professionals and human resource professionals in the service and manufacturing sectors network, matching college graduates with potential employers.

American Council on International Personnel

http://www.ahrm.org/acip/acip.htm

Focuses on movement of personnel over international borders, providing conferences and seminars, newletters, an immigration hotline, a job referral service and an Exchange Visitor program.

American Marketing Association
http://www.ama.org

Provides information and education to marketing professionals in business.

American Productivity and Quality Center
http://www.apqc.org

A non-profit organization dedicated to helping companies find and adopt best practices.

American Society for Industrial Security
http://www.asisonline.org

Organization of security professionals presents latest developments in security practice and technology for development and management of security programs.

American Society for Quality Control
http://www.asqc.org

Presents information on process improvement, teamwork, and quality standards.

American Society for Training and Development
http://www.astd.org

Professional organization for professionals involved in workplace training and performance provides leadership in achieving work competence, peformance and fulfillment. Site offers information on over one dozen human resources associations.

American Society of Pension Actuaries
http://www.aspa.org

The ASPA is a professional society consisting of actuaries, consultants, administrators and other benefits professionals.

Its 3,000 members provide services to approximately 30 percent of the qualified plans in the United States. ASPA serves as a professional association to educate pension actuaries and to preserve and enhance the private pension system as part of the development of a cohesive retirement income policy.

Association for Human Resource Management
http://www.ahrm.org

Organization of human resource practitioners, compensation, benefits, training and relocation specialists.

Business Enterprise Trust
http://www.betrust.org

Promotes social leadership in business, emphasizing bold, creative leadership combining sound management and social conscience.

Employee Assistance Professionals Association
http://www.ahrm.org/eapa/eapa.htm

Assists employers, employees and family members with personal and behavioral problems adversely affecting job performance and productivity.

Employee Benefit Research Institute
http://www.ebri.org

Conducts original public policy research and education on employee benefits and economic security.

Foundation for Enterprise Development
http://www.fed.org

Helps create highly effective competitive enterprises through equity compensation, employee ownership and involvement and other high performance business strategies.

Grantsmanship Center
http://www.tgci.com

Training and funding information for the nonprofit sector.

Human Resources Institute
http:/hri.eckerd.edu/about.html

Explores over 100 personnel management topics.

Human Resources Planning Society
http://www.hrps.org/html/index1.htm

HRPS is a non-profit organization dedicated to human resource issues. Among other things, this site contains discussion groups, a searchable directory of HRPS members, a list of publications, information on upcoming workshops, and links to HR-related issues.

Industrial Relations Research Association
http://www.ilr.cornell.edu

Organization of industrial relations and human resource practitioners and academics. Provides meetings and publications.

Institute of Management and Administration
http://www.ioma.com

IOMA site offers articles, newsletters and links on a variety of business isuues.

International Association for Human Resource Information Management-USA
http://www.ihrim.org

Focuses on information systems for human resources. Formerly HRSP.

International Foundation of Employee Benefits Plans
http://www.ifebp.org

Largest educational association (with over 34,000 members) serving the employee benefits field provides an extensive array of programs and services.

International Personnel Management Association
http://ipma-hr.org

Provides reliable, valid and legally defensible entry-level and promotional examinations to public agencies.

National Association of Temporary and Staffing Services
http://www.natss.org

NATSS members are active in all types of staffing services, which include professional employer services (employee leasing), managed services (outsourcing), payrolling placement services, temporary-to-full-time services, and long-term staffing.

National Association of Workforce Professionals
http://www.work-web.com/nawdp

Association of professionals in employment, training and related areas provides resources and information.

National Employee Services and Recreation Association
http://www.ahrm.org/nesra/nesra.htm

Serves organizations and professionals who promote organizational productivity and profitability through employee services, fitness and health promotion programs.

National Institute of Pension Administrators
http://www.nipa.org

NIPA is a national association representing the retirement and employee benefit plan administration profession.

Society for Human Resource Management
http://www.shrm.org

The main human resource organization in the United States, providing publications, conferences, and seminars. Includes HR Talk, live discussion groups, HR News Online and a government affairs section.

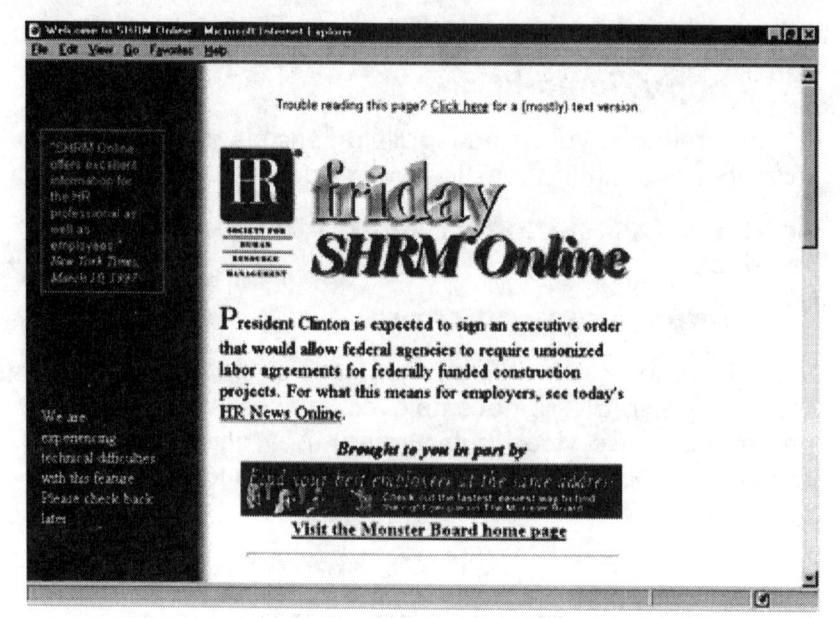

Workflow and Reengineering International Association

http://www.waria.com

Focuses on business process reengineering, workflow and electronic commerce and facilitates sharing experiences, product evaluations, education, training and networking opportunities for users and vendors.

BEHAVIOR AT WORK

Friend and Walker: Industrial Psychology

http://www.friend-walker.com

Consultants specializing in psychological testing, interviewing, and behavioral problems related to personnel management.

International Personnel Management Association Professional Journals

http://www.ipmaac.org/journals

Presents articles from recent issues of human resources, personnel, and industrial/organizational psychology journals.

Nijenrode Business Webserver for Human Resource Management & Organizational Behavior

http://www.nijenrode.nl/nbr/hrm

International research center on organizational learning, change, motivation, and empowerment.

WISSAGO

http://wissago.uwex.edu/test/joe/1987winter/a5.html

Article on Behaviorally Anchored Rating Scales, which measure behaviors, not personality. Provides raters and ratees with clear statements of performance goals, based on a thorough job analysis.

BENEFITS

Advanced Benefit Services

http://net-gate.com/~abs/abs.html

Specializing in employee benefits and communication, ABS is an employee benefit cost reduction specialist, dedicated to providing professional services to companies needing effective, cost saving employee benefits programs.

Aetna

http://www.aetna.com

Aetna provides business, life, health, and auto insurance, as well as information on retirement and financial services, and an online directory of doctors, hospitals, and other medical services.

American Dental Association

http://www.ada.org

This site offers the Dental Benefits Plan, an effective way to control the high costs of administering a dental program while at the same time providing comprehensive dental care to all employees. Direct reimbursement eliminates the overhead of outside insurers, allowing you to reimburse your employees directly for their expenses from an interest-earning fund created specifically for your company. Direct reimbursement helps assure that your employees get the services they need at a reasonable price.

American Society of Pension Actuaries
http://www.aspa.org

The ASPA is a professional society consisting of actuaries, consultants, administrators and other benefits professionals. Its 3,000 members provide services to approximately 30 percent of the qualified plans in the United States. ASPA serves as a professional association to educate pension actuaries and to preserve and enhance the private pension system as part of the development of a cohesive retirement income policy.

Benefit Design, Inc.
http://www.benefitsdesign.com/m1.htm

These employee benefits consultants and providers can assist corporations in developing a clear picture of their employee benefits needs. They offer a "corporate performance snapshot" which will assist in identifying your employee benefits philosophy and goals. It evaluates options and calculates savings. They can assist with compliance with ERISA, COBRA, and 401(K) plans.

Benefit Software, Inc.
http://www.bsiweb.com/aboutbsi.htm

BSI is a leading developer of highly specialized employee fringe benefits, communications and workers compensation case management software systems. *Fringe Facts* is an employee benefit software system that produces personalized fringe benefit statements for employers. *Comp Watch* is a workers compensation case management/claims tracking system that produces the employer's injury and illness form.

Benefit Systems Technologies
http://www.benefittechs.com

BST is a technical consulting company committed to quality client support in employee benefit processing. Their primary focus is on the implementation, upgrading, and maintenance of qualified and non-qualified defined contribution recordkeeping systems.

Benefits Advantage
http://www.business-software.com

Software organizes and automates benefits administration and other human resources processes.

BenefitsLink
http://www.benefitslink.com

Information on employee benefit plans and services, pension and profit-sharing plans. The BenefitsLink Newsletter is published via e-mail once or twice a week. Each issue contains news of important employee benefits developments and tips for using BenefitsLink and other employee benefits Internet resources. The site also has a comprehensive listing of Web sites on a range of benefits topics, from A to Z.

Blair Mill Administrators, Inc.
http://www.blairmill.com

This third-party administrator provides information for organizations that self-insure their medical benefits.

Bureau of Labor Statistics
http://stats.bls.gov:80/proghome.htm

Employee benefits survey, cost of living, and other information can be found here.

Catalog of Federal Domestic Assistance
http://www.gsa.gov/fdac/default.htm

Federal programs, projects, services and activiites which provide financial and non-financial benefits.

Cohen & Associates Agencies
http://www.cyberconnect.com/insurance

This firm offers insurance and financial services specializing in meeting the financial concerns of small business owners. Services include employer benefits, estate planning, and business succession protection.

Collin W. Fritz and Associates
http://www.pension-specialists.com/index.htm

CWF is one of the country's leading IRA and pension consulting service firms. They offer the most complex package of IRA and pension forms and supporting services, including IRA compliance, training (live and videotape), periodical publications, workplace reference manuals, software and auditing services.

CORE, Inc.
http://www.coreinc.com

Information on disability management services is available at this site.

Cornell University
http://www.law.edu

Information on workers' compensation law is available at this site.

Cyborg: Quality Options in Human Resource Technology
http://www.cyborg.com

Benefits administration software provider. Also offers software solutions for payroll, time and attendance, and other human resource applications.

DATAIR Employee Benefit Systems, Inc.
http://www.datair.com

Pension and benefits software and services. Site includes reports, documents, product demonstrations and links to other benefits sites on the Web.

E-Benefits
http://www.e-benefits.com/aboutus.htm

E-Benefits offers clients integrated human resource administration solutions for insurance selection, payroll processing, retirement plan administration, legal and regulatory compliance, and employee recordkeeping.

Employee Assistance Professionals Association
http://www.ahrm.org/eapa/eapa.htm

Assists employers, employees and family members with personal and behavioral problems adversely affecting job performance and productivity.

Employee Benefit Research Institute
http://www.ebri.org

Health insurance benefit information. EBRI is dedicated to advancing the public's understanding of employee benefits.

Fidelity Investments
http://www.fidelityatwork.com

Fidelity is a brokerage firm that can help HR deparments set up 401(K) savings plans and other financial packages.

Gay Workplace Issues
http://www.nyu.edu/pages/sls/gaywork

Information on policies and issues surrounding gay men and women in the workforce. Coverage includes discussion of benefits for unmarried partners and lists of relevant organizations.

Health and Human Services Agencies
http://www.os.dhhs.gov

This site has a list of federal agencies and their services.

HR Investment Consultants

http://www.401ksearch.com

This is an online service which allows employers to search for the best 401(K) providers based on their specific needs.

Information Technology Support Center

http://www.itsc.state.md.us

Information on unemployment insurance, including management, data and statistics.

Interactive Corp.

http://www.interactivecorp.com

Customized systems organize, update and present benefits and company information over an Intranet.

International Foundation of Employee Benefit Plans

http://www.ifebp.org

Industry news, publications, seminars, conferences and other services from the largest educational association serving the employee benefits field.

National Institute of Pension Administrators
http://www.nipa.org

NIPA is a national association representing the retirement and employee benefit plan administration profession.

Pension and Benefits
http://www.riatax.com/washdc.html

Research Institute of America publishes pension and benefits information to keep HR professionals up-to-date on new developments or changes in this area. It also has information on estate planning and federal taxes.

Pension Benefit Guaranty Corporation
http://www.pbgc.gov

The PBGC mission is to protect the retirement incomes of nearly 42 million American workers. Their site offers frequently asked questions, publications, and a variety of technical information to help keep you informed about pension issues.

Reinhart, Boenner, Van Deuren, Nomis & Rieselbach
http://www.rbvdnr.com/eb/eb-main.htm

This is an employee benefits law firm that has served the human resources field for four decades. The firm has one of the largest employee benefits practices in the country, with clients in 40 states.

Retirement Plans for the Self-Employed
http://www.benefitslink.com/forms/pub560.html

This site will tell HR people how to set up a Keough plan. Keough plans are tax qualified retirement plans sponsored by sole proprietors who are self-employed.

Rocky Mountain Employee Benefits Bulletin
http://www.rmeb.com/bulletin/index.html

A quarterly publication on benefits-related stories from Rocky Mountain Employee Benefits. They also provide consulting services to tailor a retirement plan to meet your company's needs, including 401(K) plans.

Social Security Administration

http://www.ssa.gov/programs/retirement/ publications/retirement.html

Information on retirement benefits and eligibility requirements.

State of Wisconsin

http://badger.state.wi.us/agencies/ dilhr/wc/wcother.html

http://badger.state.wi.us/agencies/ dilhr/wc/wcdesc.html

Links to all state workers' compensation administration agencies and information on writing injury descriptions.

SunGard Employee Benefit Systems

http://www.sungardebs.com

Provider of software and services for benefits recordkeeping for 401(k) and defined contribution plans.

Towers Perrin Online

http://www.towersperrin.com

Focuses on international compensation and benefit issues, emerging trends, new legislation and other developments in major countries.

Travis

http://www.travisoft.com

Systems for administration of flexible benefit plans (cafeteria, 'full flex' and flexible spending accounts).

Watson Wyatt Insider

http://www.watsonwyatt.com/homepage/ usane.htm

This is a monthly compilation of regulations, policy and research about benefits, retirement, and other human resource issues.

Wharton School of the University of Pennsylvania

http://prc.wharton.upenn.edu/prc/prc.html

The Wharton School is committed to generating debate on key policy issues affecting pensions and other employee benefits.

William M. Mercer, Inc.

http://www.mercer.com/mercer/hr/ibg/index.html

Employee benefits and human resource consulting firm specializing in healthcare, group insurance, flexible benefits, compensation and retirement.

BUSINESS INFORMATION

Access Business OnLine

http://www.clickit.com/touch/home.html

Access Business OnLine offers fast breaking news, searchable editorial archives, corporate news wires and press releases. Classified advertising and requests for bids, forums and news groups, company profiles, directories, trade show listings, conferences, seminars, and information from associations are included.

Dun & Bradstreet

http://www.dnb.com

Dun & Bradstreet is recognized around the world as the leader in providing business information to customers. D&B evaluates and analyzes business information. If there is a business out there, D&B has that data.

Hoover Business Profiles

http://www.pathfinder.com

Provides information on most major U.S. companies.

List of Top 1000 US Companies

http://techweb.cmp.com/ia/hot1000/hot1.html.

This site has links to the top 1,000 American companies with Web sites.

Sales Leads USA

http://www.abii.com

Addresses and phone numbers for every business in the nation, along with business profiles.

Thomas Register

http://www.thomasregister.com/index.html

Search 155,000 U.S. and Canadian companies to find the products or services you need. Thomas Register is the world's largest online industrial buying source.

World Wide Web Yellow Pages

http://www.mcp.com/18828596272043/nrp/wwwyp

You can look up any company, Web site or search by category. Just type in a keyword and it will find it.

COMPENSATION

Abbott, Langer & Associates Management Consultants

http://www.abbott-langer.com

View and or purchase compensation and benefits reports.

Again Technologies

http://www.againtech.com

This site provides information on software and consulting to help administer profit sharing, sales commission, executive compensation, and incentive compensation plans.

American Compensation Association
http://www.acaonline.org

This non-profit association's 23,000 members design, implement, and manage employee compensation and benefits programs.

Bureau of Labor Statistics
http://stats.bls.gov:80/proghome.htm

This Department of Labor site provides data on employer costs for employee compensation, the percentage of costs associated with benefits, the costs for full-time versus part-time students, compensation costs by region, compensation and working conditions, employment cost trends, and surveys and programs on employment and unemployment, prices and living conditions, productivity, and technology.

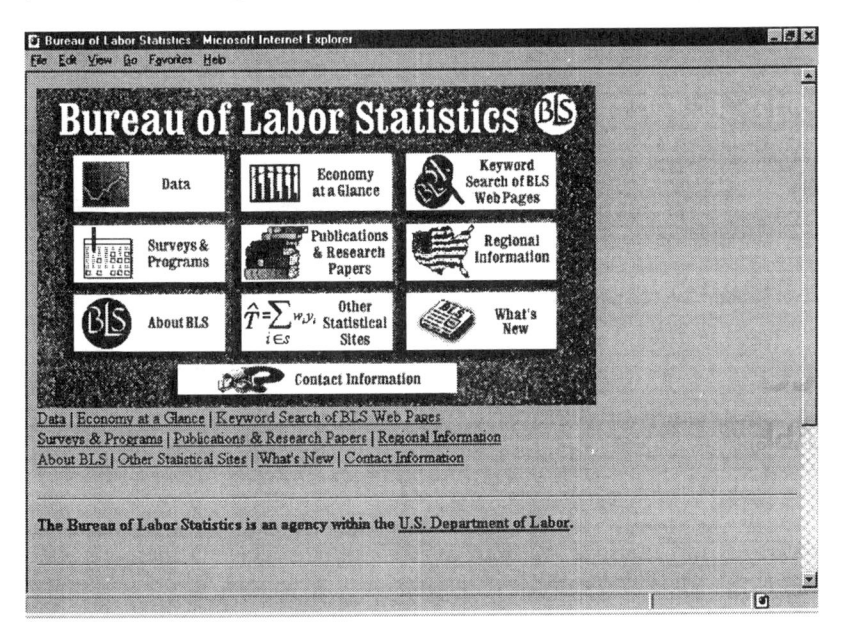

Compensation Planning Software
http://www.crl.com/~clwallis

Clayton Wallis offers integrated compensation planning systems for management.

Home Buyers Fair

http://www.homefair.com/

Use this tool to compare the cost of living in hundreds of cities in the US and abroad. This is especially valuable when dealing with employee relocation.

Human Resources Plaza

http://hodes.com/hr_plaza/hr_11.html

This site provides links to Web sites that publish salary information for human resources professionals.

Interactive Salary Survey

http://www.pencomsi.com/industry.html

PenCom has compiled a survey which lists the average salaries in all major fields. By clicking on the choices corresponding to geography, industry, years of experience, position and technical experience, it will provide the expected salary range of an employee.

JobSmart

http://www.jobsmart.org/tools/salary/surv-gen.htm

Provides average salaries offered to recent college graduates in a variety of fields, from an annual survey by the National Association of Colleges and Employers.

Montara Connection

http://www.crl.com/~beck/montara/montara.html

Montara helps companies build market-based compensation systems to attract and retain a motivated and skilled workforce. Services include job evaluation, market pricing, salary surveys, performance planning and appraisal, merit budgeting, skill-based pay, and sales incentives.

Salary Guides

http://www.espan.com/salary

Provides salary information for the computer, engineering, accounting, and finance professions.

Salary Information/Salary Survey Sites
http://www.hodes.com/hr_plaza/hr_11.html

Tools for determining salaries in a range of industries.

Society for Human Resource Management
http://www.shrm.org

Provides education and information services, conferences, and seminars on compensation and othr issues for human resources professionals.

COUNSELING SERVICES

Partnership Group
http://www.tpglifebalance.com

A consultation and referral service designed to help employees balance personal and professional responsibilities.

DEVELOPMENT

Academy of Human Resource Development
http://www.ahrd.org

The Academy was formed to encourage systematic study of human resources development, theories, processes, and practices to disseminate information about HRD research findings and to provide opportunities for social interaction among those interested in human resource development.

American Society for Training and Development
http://www.astd.org

Professional organization for professionals involved in workplace training and performance provides leadership in achieving work competence, peformance and fulfillment. Site offers information on over one dozen human resources associations.

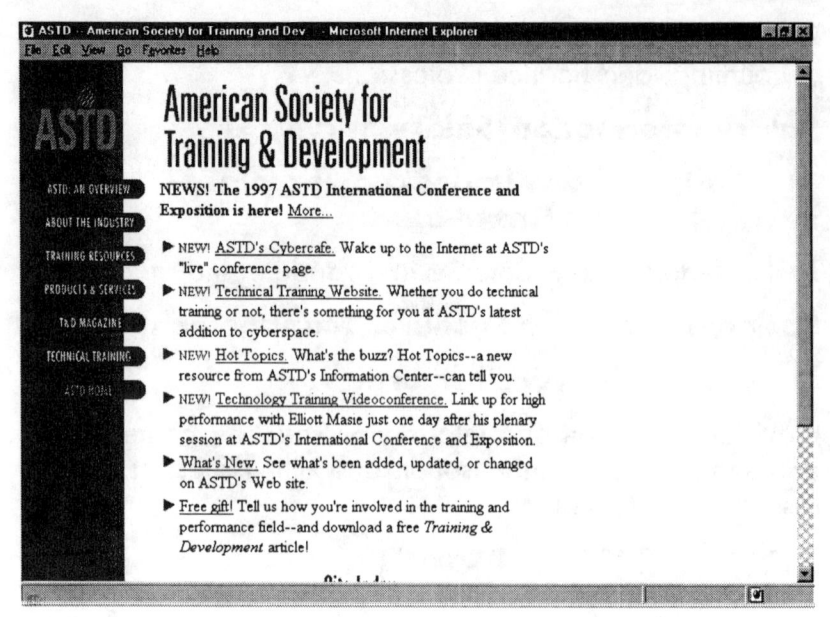

Development Dimensions International

http://www.ddiworld.com

Consulting firm helps clients improve business performance by aligning people strategies with business strategies.

HR Press Software

http://www.hrpress-software.com/index.html

Describes software for employee training and development.

Human Resource Development Network

http://www.mcb.co.uk/hrn/nethome.htm

Human Resource Development Network is an online service designed to help those working in the field of HRD and support trying to implement initiatives within their organization.

Personnel & Development Network

http://www.pdn.co.uk/pdn.html

PDN offers professionals easily accessible information on many specialties within the human resource field at one central Internet address. It has a huge database of companies that cover testing and assessment, employee benefits, employee relations, occupational health and safety, conferences and exhibits, training, recruitment, and employment law.

Training and Development Resource Center
http://www.tcm.com/trdev

Information and links on suppliers and materials on training, distance learning, and development.

TRDEVL (Training and Development List)
http://www.intrack.com/intranet

Discussion group facilitates communication between training and development scholars and practioners.

DISABILITY

Americans with Disabilities Act
http://www.usdoj.gov/crt/ada/adahom1.htm

ADA resources provided by the US Department of Justice on this site include reports, press releases, and information on settlements, technical assistance programs, and litigation projects.

Berger Law Office
http://www.rkb.com

This site provides links which facilitate legal research on such topics as the ADA and employment law.

CORE, Inc.
http://www.coreinc.com

Information on disability management services is available at this site.

Court TV
http://www.courttv.com/seminars/handbook/adaprimr.html

Information on the types of organizations which must comply with the Americans with Disabilities Act is available at this site.

Disability Etiquette Handbook

http://www.ci.sat.tx.us/planning/hand book

Suggestions for expanding opportunities for people with disabilities to pursue their careers and independent lifestyles.

Employee Relations Web Picks

http://www.nyper.com

Links are provided to Web sites covering the Americans with Disabilities Act, affirmative action, and employment law.

Equal Opportunity Publications

http://www.eop.com/ccwd/homepage.html

EOP has a career center for workforce diversity. They publish magazines entitled *Careers and the Disabled*, *Equal Opportunity*, and *Workforce Diversity*.

Find Law—Labor Law

http://www.findlaw.com

Human resources professionals can find information on their responsibilities under the Americans with Disabilities Act at this site.

Job Accomodation Network

http://janweb.icdi.wvu.edu

Learn how many companies are modifying their recruitment and selection processes in order to comply with the Americans with Disabilities Act. Provides examples of areas affected by the ADA. Information on job accomodations for employability of people with disabilities is this site's focus.

NCSA Mosaic Access Page

http://bucky.aa.uic.edu

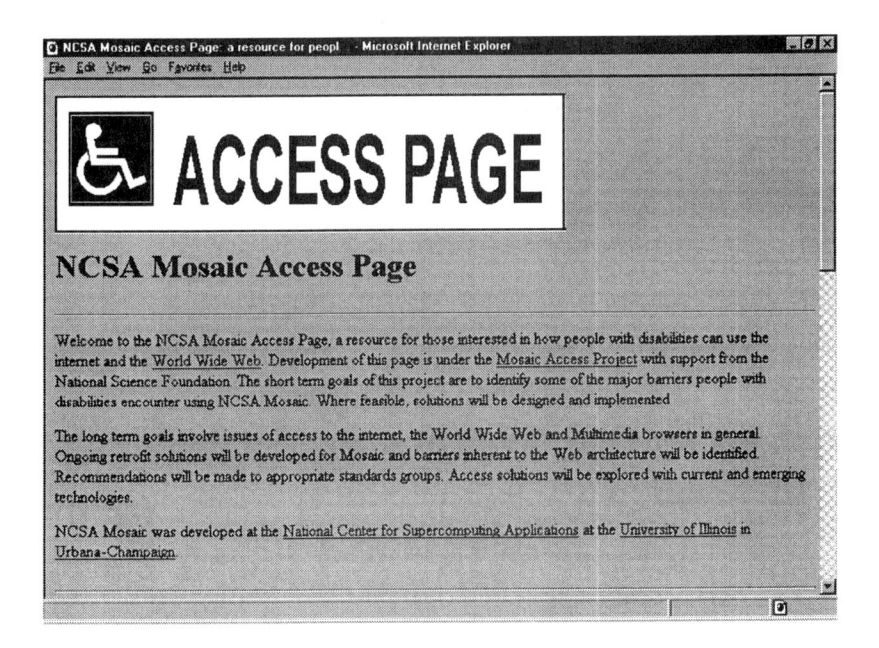

Identifies major barriers encountered by people with disabilities, along with how design and implement solutions. Includes information on how the disabled can use the Internet and World Wide Web.

DIVERSITY

Equal Opportunity Publications

> http://www.eop.com/ccwd/homepage.html

EOP has a career center for workforce diversity affirmative action, diversity recruitment for minorities, women and people with disabilities. EOP publishes career magazines entitled *Workforce Diversity, Equal Opportunity, Women Engineer, Minority Engineer,* and *Careers and the Disabled.*

Griggs Productions, Inc.

> http://www.griggs.com

Site features *No Potential Lost*, a software program that clarifies of how diversity, relationship and cultural dynamics affect performance in the workplace.

Saludos Web
http://www.saludos.com

This Web site is dedicated to promoting Hispanic careers and education.

SER Jobs for Progress National
http://www.sernational.org

This site's special emphasis is on the needs of Hispanics in education, job skill training, employment, and literacy.

University of Maryland Diversity Database
http://www.inform.umd.edu/EdRes/Topic

This site contains definitions, issue-specific resources, general diversity resources, diversity plans, statements, and initiatives on diversity from various institutions.

EMPLOYEE OWNERSHIP

Foundation for Enterprise Development
http://www.fed.org

Helps create highly effective competitive enterprises through equity compensation, employee ownership and involvement and other high performance business strategies.

National Center for Employee Ownership
http://www.nceo.org

The NCEO is a private, non-profit membership and information organization. Supported by its members, it serves as the leading source of accurate, unbiased information on employee stock ownership plans (ESOPs) and other forms of employee ownership.

EMPLOYEE RELATIONS

All Business Network
http://www.all-biz.com/8pts.htm

This site helps identify and correct the most common employment relations problems, like including inappropriate material in employee handbooks, having inadequate or nonexistent job descriptions, waiting too long to discharge employees, and not evaluating job performance.

Alternative Dispute Resolution

http://www.adr.org/guide/html

Does your organization use alternatives to litigation for resolving disputes? This site will help you explore arbitration and mediation options.

Caras & Associates, Inc.

http://www.carasadr.com

Information on alternative dispute resolution, an increasingly popular alternative for resolving employer/employee disputes.

Communications Briefings

http://www.combriefings.com/welcome.html

Practical tips and proven tactics for improvings all types of communications, spurring productivity, improving teamwork, and motivating employees.

Court TV

http://www.courttv.com/seminars/handbook/unions.html

Many employers fail to realize that they have a legal right to advise their employees of the organization's opinion that a union is not in the employees' best interest. See this site for details.

Employee Relations Web Picks

http://www.nyper.com

Topics covered include labor relations, affirmative action, the Americans with Disabilities Act, collective bargaining, and employment law.

Focus Groups

http://www.uth.tmc.edu:80/ut_general/admin_fin/cqi/resource/tools/cusgrp.html

This site contains information on how to conduct a focus group.

HR Magazine

http://www.shrm.org/hrmagazine

This site offers current and past articles from this monthly magazine.

HRNET Discussion Group

http://www.aom.pace.edu/lists/l-hrnet.html

Exchange questions and answers about human resources problems and solution with 3,000 colleagues from around the world.

Institute of Collective Bargaining—Cornell University

http://www.ilr.cornell.edu/depts/icb

Briefing papers and a newsletter on collective bargaining are available at this Web site.

Online Career Center

http://www.occ.com

This site provides information on downsizing and the use of outplacement services to help employees reestablish career goals and secure new employment. Includes advice on working with outplacement services and what to expect from professional counselors.

Society for Human Resource Management

http://www.shrm.org/

SHRM represents the interests of over 79,000 human resource professionals worldwide, providing members with education and information publications and services, conferences, seminars, and government and media representation.

Strategic Communications Online
http://www.tagonline.com/~strategy

Offers support for professionals and organizations on business communications issues.

Technology, HR & Communication Home Page
http://www.inforamp.net/~bcroft

Information on new and emerging technologies for communications.

3 Ring Information Systems
http://www.3ring.com

This firm provides companies with electronic publishing tools for communicating human resource information to employees via a user-friendly interface. Their services include editing, organizing, indexing and presenting company materials, policies and procedures, benefits, financial plans, safety, and security.

EMPLOYMENT DISCRIMINATION

Americans with Disabilities Act
http://www.usdoj.gov/crt/ada/adahom1.htm

ADA resources provided by the US Department of Justice on this site include reports, press releases, and information on settlements, technical assistance programs, and litigation projects.

Berkshire Associates
http://www.berkshire-aap.com

Software program facilitates affirmative action programs, handling statistical reports and data.

Disability Etiquette Handbook

http://www.ci.sat.tx.us/planning/handbook

Suggestions for expanding opportunities for people with disabilities to pursue their careers and independent lifestyles.

Gay Workplace Issues

http://www.nyu.edu/pages/sls/gaywork

Information on policies and issues surrounding gay men and women in the workforce. Coverage includes discussion of benefits for unmarried partners and lists of relevant organizations.

Job Accomodation Network

http://janweb.icdi.wvu.edu

Job accomodations for employability of people with disabilities is this site's focus.

NCSA Mosaic Access Page

http://bucky.aa.uic.edu

Identifies major barriers encountered by people with disabilities, along with how to design and implement solutions. Includes information on how the disabled can use the Internet and World Wide Web.

SER Jobs for Progress National

http://www.sernational.org

This site's special emphasis is on the needs of Hispanics in education, job skill training, employment, and literacy.

US Department of Labor Women's Bureau

http://www.dol.gov/dol/wb

Information presented on this site includes fact sheets about women in the workplace and statistics on earning differences between men and women.

ERGONOMICS

Carpal Tunnel Syndrome Page
http://www.netaxs.com/~iris/cts/welcome.html

Prevention strategies for CTDs, including exercises.

CTDNews Online
http://ctdnews.com

Information on ergonomic products, inlcuding speech recognition systems, handtools, keyboards, software, and furniture.

Ergoware Products
http://www.nmia.com/ergoware

Information on ergonomic products, including wrist and foot supports, seating, and software.

ErgoWeb
http://www.ergoweb.com

Information on ergonomic analysis tools, case studies, standards and guidelines.

National Institute of Occupational Safety and Health
http://www.cdc.gov/niosh/homepage.html

The federal agency which conducts safety and industrial hygiene research presents lists of publications and videos available, as well as fact sheets on indoor air quality, back belts, and carpal tunnel syndrome.

UVA's Video Display Ergonomics Page
http://www.virginia.edu/~enhealth/ERGONOMICS/toc.html

Covers office ergonomics topics including video display terminal use, the use of stretch breaks for computer users and back injury prevention.

GENERAL

Biz

http://www.thebiz.co.uk/humtdetcc_m.htm

This site covers human resources, training, and development. Within each subject area, there are many links to other Websites on those specific areas.

Duke University Human Resources

http://www.hr.duke.edu

This site features information on training, manuals, guides, handbooks, and human resource information systems.

George Mason University

http://hr.gmu.edu

This site offers good human resource policies and procedures, newsletters, benefits, training, recruitment, payroll, forms, and materials.

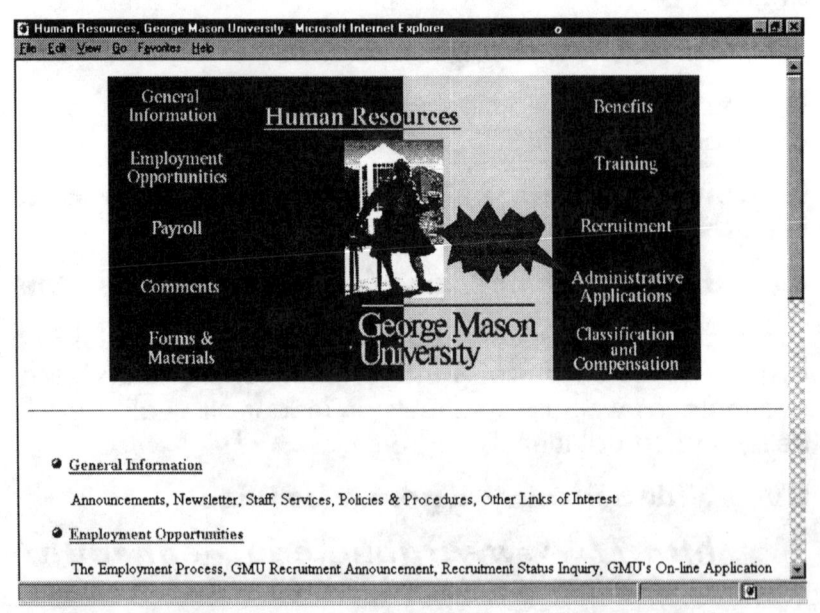

North Carolina Human Resource Center

http://www.webcom.com/~nccareer/hrctr.html

This site offers HR professionals a wide range of information concerning human resource issues, such as recruiting, selection and assessment, compensation and benefits, employee relations, training, and legal compliance.

Personnel & Development Network

http://www.pdn.co.uk/pdn.html

PDN offers professionals easily accessible information on many specialties within the human resource field at one central Internet address. It has a huge database of companies that cover testing and assessment, employee benefits, employee relations, occupational health and safety, conferences and exhibits, training, recruitment, and employment law.

US Human Resources

http://www.value-link.com/ushrng.html

This site has many listings for seminars, performance management courses, training, career transition assessment, reorganization placement assistance, alternative dispute systems, how to determine sexual harassment in your office, computerized leadership assessment and custom course design.

HEALTH PROMOTION

Association for Worksite Health Promotion

http://www.awhp.com/#anchor322033

Helps companies determine if corporate fitness programs are good investments. Suggests techniques and best practices.

Depaul University

http://condor.depaul.edu/ethics/sun23.html

Presents information on company AIDS prevention programs.

Dreyfuss Hunt

http://www.toptopics.com

A library of health, wellness, safety, productivity, motivation, and stress articles. These ready-to-use articles and other features can be purchased with the click of a mouse and immediately downloaded for use in company newsletters, employee newsletters, or intranets.

The full-length articles can be searched by topic, title, key word, seasonality, and word count. Each article is updated regularly and users are free to add, modify or customize them. Articles can be reproduced in print or posted electronically. Before purchasing by credit card (encrypted for safety), users see a short description, word count and price for each article. Upon purchase, the complete article appears on the user's screen.

Hazelden

http://www.hazelden.com

This site created by a non-profit organization helping people recovering from alcohol and drug addiction explains the dangers that use of controlled substances can pose to employees.

Health Care Financing Administration

http://www.hcfa.gov

The HCFA is the federal agency that administers the Medicare and Medicaid programs. It is also one of the primary sources of data on containing health care costs.

Plainfield

http://www.plainfiled.bypass.com/~twilbur/calorie.html

Page discusses daily caloric needs.

Process Therapy Institute

http://www.processes.org/stress.html

This site offers a stress test and explains how quality of life affects productivity.

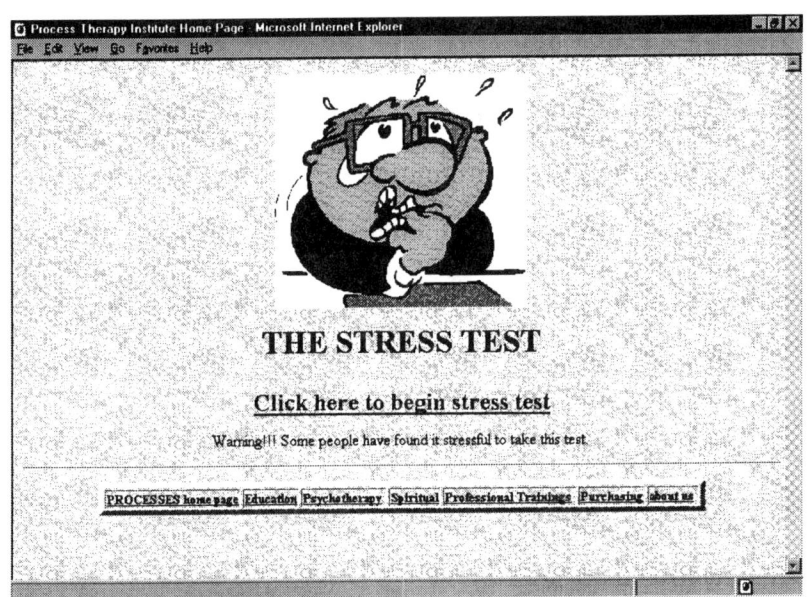

University of Alberta

http://www.geog.ualberta.ca/als/alswp4.html

An article on leisure's relationship to health and how recreational activities can help control rising healthcare costs.

University of California/Berkeley

http://server.berkeley.edu/dailycal/issues/09.27.95/smoking.txt

Article discusses risks of second-hand smoke and how to manage the conflicts between smokers and non-smokers in the work environment.

US Department of Agriculture

http://www.nalusda.gov/fnic/dga/dguide95.html

Explains how to start an Eat Healthy campaign at work. Explains why employers should be concerned with employees' diets and provides dietary guidelines.

US Department of Health and Human Services

http://www.os.dhhs.gov

This site covers information on many consumer-oriented health issues.

Welltech Worksite Health Promotion Program
http://www.welltech.com/programs/

Provides sample policies from the American Heart Association, Blue Cross/Blue Shield, Coors Brewing Company, Mass Mutual, 3M, and Warner Lambert/Parke-Davis.

World Health Organization
http://www.who.ch

Presents information on health from a global perspective.

You First Health Risk Assessment
http://www.youfirst.com

A free, confidential health risk assessment is available to workers on the World Wide Web. The You First Health Risk Assessment employs the interactive capabilities of the Web to create an immediate individual health risk profile. Answers to questions about family history, health habits and lifestyle behaviors are analyzed to create a personal health status report that includes recommendations to improve health and minimize potential future health problems.

Internet users respond to a detailed health questionnaire that takes about five minutes to complete. You First is capable of comparing a person's "body age" with his or her chronological age. Through statistical analysis a person's lifestyle risks are evaluated against documented outcomes associated with those risks. The interactive capability of You First enables users to find how lifestyle changes can add years to a projected life span, helping workers understand how to lead healthier lives.

INTRANETS

Bernard Hodes Advertising
http://www.hodes.com

Recruitment ad firm offering intranet/Internet solutions.

Complete Intranet Resource
http://www.intrack.com/intranet/

This site offers supplier links, discussion groups, simple introductory material for new intranet users, and an internal search engine. One exclusive feature: a help desk that accepts your questions and posts the answers for all to see.

Intranet Journal
http://www.intranetjournal.com

This site from Brill Editorial is a good place for human resource professionals to learn how companies are using intranets. The moderated discussions, which contain hundreds of messages, allow you to exchange information with people from many disciplines including technical professionals who build intranets and other human resources managers who set policies for intranet use. A sample discussion topic: Should HR departments screen intranet documents before employees post them? There are also many links to intranet suppliers.

JOB SEARCH SKILLS

Amsquare
http://www.amsquare.com/america/career14.html

Helps job seekers learn how to emphasize the strengths (leadership, flexibility, resourcefulness, etc.) that will attract a prospective employer.

Career Atlas for the Road
http://www.isdn.net/nis

Frequently asked questions, resumés, and other information on careers.

Career Crafting
http:/www.well.com/user/careerc

Helps users evaluate current employment and determine whether another job would be more desirable.

Career Dynamics

http://www.careerdynamics.com

This workforce consulting firm specializing in transition and organizational transformation issues presents information on current topics human resource managers are dealing with, techniques for communicating employment opportunities, Career Partners International (a provider of career and workforce management services), and links to other HR sites.

Career Magazine

http://www.careermag.com

A comprehensive resource for job seekers, updated with valuable new information daily.

Career Management International

http://www.cmi.com

This site offers a variety of links for career professionals.

Career Mart

http://www.careermart.com

An online job fair offering job listings and company information searchable by location, job and other variables.

Career Planning Process

http://www.bgsu.edu/offices/careers/process/process.html

A career planing and competency model helps individuals explore information, gain competencies, make decisions, set goals and take action.

CareerPath

http://www.careerpath.com

Employment ads from seventeen major cities are presented on this site.

Career Shop

http://www.careershop.com

Online database of resumés and employment opportunities.

Career Web

http://www.cweb.com

Job listings and a resumé pool are among the tools found at this job search site.

Collegegrad

http://www.collegegrad.com/intv/dress.html

General guidelines for interview success, including how to dress appropriately for the jobs candidates are applying for.

DejaNews

http://www.dejanews.com

Find newsgroups on any topic of interest and view articles from newsgroups.

ERIC Clearinghouse on Adult, Career and Vocational Education

http://www.coe.ohio-state.edu/cete/ericacve/index.htm

Information, publications and services on all aspects of career, vocational and technical education, including workforce preparation.

E-SPAN—Online Employment Connection

http://www.espan.com/docs
http://www.espan.com/docs/telefon.html
http://www.espan.com/docs/rich2.html
http://www.espan.com/docs/rich4.html
http://www.espan.com/docs/intprac.html

Includes resumé, interviewing and salary guides, occupational outlook handbook, information and advice on telephone skills, and provides tips on networking techniques and preparing for reference checks.

FedWorld Federal Jobs Announcement Search

http://www.fedworld.gov/jobs/jobsearch.html

Database of US government job postings, updated daily and searchable by location.

Illinois Employment and Training Center

http://www.apage.com/host/ietcitt.html

Offers free professional personnel services to employers and job seekers.

Interviewing Skills

http://www.safetynet.doleta.gov/intrview.htm

Interview advice and common interview questions.

Kaplan Career Center

http://www.kaplan.com

Provides assistance in determining career options, job selection criteria, and career trends.

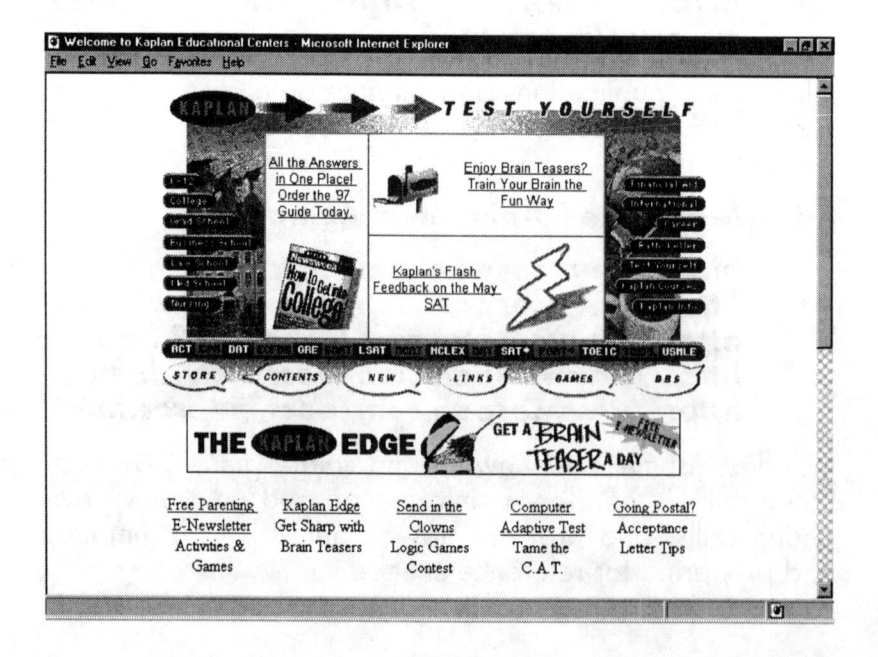

Mayo Online Career Center
http://www.mayo.edu/career/ keywords.html

Helps job seekers identify job skills and add keywords that describe skills to their resumes.

Monster Board
http://www.monster.com

Free access to over 50,000 job listings.

Netsmart
http://www.netsmart.com/flesher/tips.html

Article entitled "Resume Tips" helps job seekers identify their accomplishments and build winning resumes.

New York State Department of Labor
http://www.labor.state.ny.us

Wage, workforce and labor market information for employers, career resources library, NY Job Bank, training, retraining and unemployment insurance information for employees.

News Flashes
http://www.jobweb.org/cohrma/ chornews.htm

News releases, articles, and reviews of books on employee benefits, relocation, jobs for recent college graduates, etc.

Online Career Center
http://www.occ.com

This non-profit career resource is the Internet's most frequently accessed career site.

Planning Your Future—Federal Employee's Survival Guide
http://www.safetynet.doleta.gov

Information on starting a new career, preparing a job search, choosing a career, resumés and cover letters, job opportunities, and interviewing skills.

Purdue Online Writing Laboratory Resumé Workshop

http://owl.english.purdue.edu/files/resume.html

Resumé information and advice on job hunting.

Recruiters Online Network

http://www.ipa.com

Send resumés to recruiting and employment professionals or review employer profiles and contact them directly.

Resumix

http://www.resumix.com/resume/resume-form.html

A fill-in-the-blanks resumé writing site.

Sales Leads USA

http://www.abii.com

Addresses and phone numbers for every business in the nation, along with business profiles.

SER Jobs for Progress National

http://www.sernational.org

Human resource development, with emphasis on Hispanic education, job skill training, literacy and employment needs.

US Department of Labor

http://www.dol.gov

America's Job Bank and minimum wage information.

Westech Career Expo

http://www.vjf.com/pub/westech

A resume database and listing of job fairs are offered.

What Color is Your Parachute? Job Hunting Online

http://www.washingtonpost.com/parachute

Site based on best-selling job search book.

WINGS—The Interactive Network of Government Services

http://www.wings.gov

Services and information from all areas of government, including jobs, health, moving, and retirement.

Worknet Job Search

http://www.worknet.ca

Canadian employment opportunities online.

LABOR-MANAGEMENT RELATIONS

AFL-CIO LaborWeb

http://www.aflcio.org

Policy statements and press releases from labor unions.

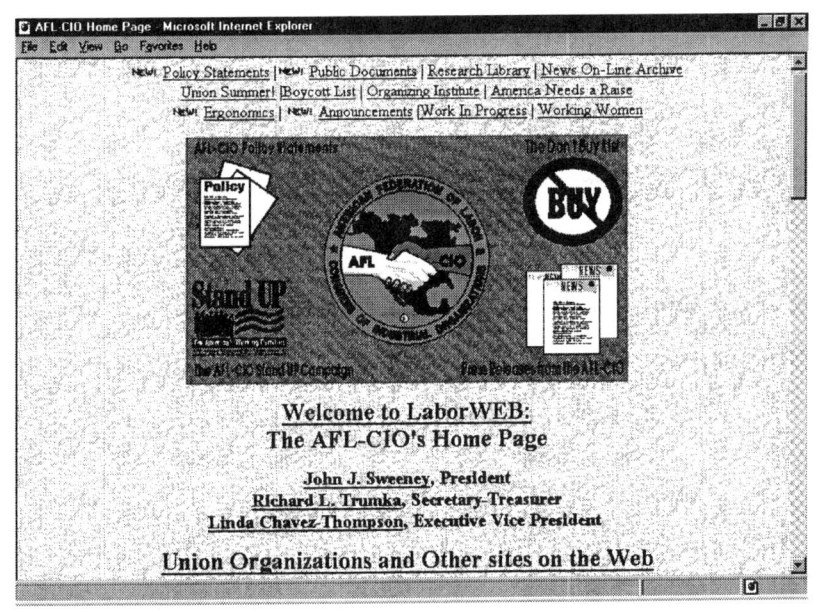

Cornell Institute of Collective Bargaining

http://www.ilr.cornell.edu/depet/icb

Cornell University School of Industrial and Labor Relations

http://www.ilr.cornell.edu

Information on all aspects of employer-employee relations and workplace issues.

Cornell Work and Environment Initiative

http://www.cfe.cornell.edu/wei

Provides information on labor-management relations, human resource management and industrial hygiene from the perspective of management, unions, and government.

Court TV

http://www.courttv.com/seminars/handbook/unions.html

Many employers fail to realize that they have a legal right to advise their employees of the organization's opinion that a union is not in the employees' best interest. See this site for details.

Foundation for Enterprise Development
http://www.fed.org

Information on equity compensation, and employee ownership and involvement can be found at this site.

Liszt Email Discussion Group Directory
http://www.liszt.com

This Web site includes conflict resolution and industrial relations listservs, newsgroups, and bulletin boards.

National Labor Relations Board
http://www.nlrb.gov

Information on the laws governing relations between labor unions and employers involved in interstate commerce.

People Tech
http://www.peopletech.com/ppl

Information on the human relations aspects of implementing large scale change in business strategy, practices, and corporate structure.

Union Resource Network
http://www.unions.org/URN

Index of union websites.

US Companies That Are Doing It Right
http://www.fed.org/uscompanies

Case studies and profiles of companies cited by the US Department of Labor for exemplary ethics and responsibility.

LAWS AND REGULATIONS

All Business Network
http://www.all-biz.com/ot.htm

Information and advice on employee work break rules can be found at this site.

American Association for Affirmative Action
http://www.fga.com/aaaa

This site is dedicated to the advancement of affirmative action, equal opportunity, and the elimination of discrimination, providing information to help HR managers comply with regulations and policies.

American Psychological Association
http://www.apa.org/pubinfo/harass.html

Facts and myths about sexual harrassment are presented here to increase human resource professionals' ability to deal with these issues.

Berger Law Office
http://www.rkb.com

This site provides links which facilitate legal research on such topics as the ADA and employment law.

Cornell University Legal Information Institute
http://www.law.cornell.edu

Information on a vast array of legal isues can be found at this site.

Court TV
http://www.courttv.com/seminars/handbook/adaprimr.html

Information on the types of organizations which must comply with the Americans with Disabilities Act is available.

Employee Relations
http://www.nyper.com

Affirmative action law site that covers affirmative action, the Americans with Disabilties Act, collective bargaining, employment law, labor relations, and personnel management.

Find Law—Labor Law
http://www.findlaw.com

Human resources professionals can find information here on regulations affecting their legal responsibilities, including OSHA and ADA. This site contains a directory of legal resources featuring everything from statutes to law firms to consultants.

Government Printing Office
http://www.access.gpo.gov/su_docs/aces/aaces001.html

Search the Federal Register for Federal laws, including those covering the prohibition of employment discrimination.

Human Resource Law Website
http://www.gttlaw.com

The law firm of Greenberg, Trister & Turner specializes in human resource practice. As legal advisors to corporations and individuals, they provide a wide range of solutions to HR issues, from the relocation of personnel and contractual relations to employment policies and procedures.

Library of Congress
http://thomas.loc.gov/

Recent bills and amendments being considered by Congress can be found at this site.

National Labor Relations Board
http://www.doc.gov/nlrb/homepg.html

Information on the laws governing relations between labor unions and employers involved in interstate commerce.

Search United States Government Documents
http://www.access.gpo.gov/su_docs/aces/aaces001.html

This is a searchable database where you can find the full text of any Federal Register documents.

Small Business Law Center

http://www.courttv.com

Information resource for a range of laws and regulations.

State of Kentucky

http://www.state.ky.us

Use this site to search employment regulations and practices by state, including equal employment opportunity statutes, which may be more comprehensive than Federal laws.

US Department of Justice

http://www.usdoj.gov

Turn to the Justice Department Web site for definitive information and guidance on the Americans with Disabilities Act and many other workplace issues.

US House of Representatives Internet Law Library

http://law.house.gov

Code of Federal Regulations

http://law.house.gov/cfr.htm#search

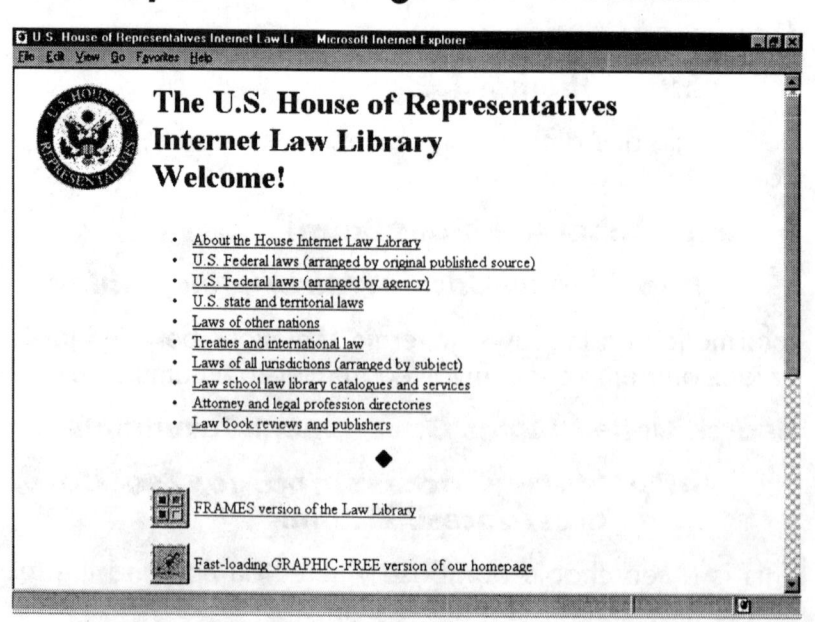

This is a comprehensive source of information regarding US and international law. The Code of Federal Regulations contains the text of government regulations issued by the agencies of the Federal government. These are final rules that have the full effect of law.

US Immigration for Canadian Businesses and Professionals

http://www.grasmick.com

Contains information about temporary and permanent US immigration work permits for Canadian citizens.

When You Have to Let Someone Go

http://www.nolo.com/nn206.html

This is an article on firing an employee. It has always been an uncomfortable task, but it used to be clear-cut and relatively free of legal complications. Things are more complicated now. Firing someone - even a person who is demonstrably incompetent - can be a risky endeavor. Do it for the wrong reason or in the wrong way and you can be obligated to pay substantial damages. This article will help reduce your chances of a former employee suing your business and winning.

White House

http://library.whitehouse.gov/ ?request=executiveorder

The president issues executive orders to insure federal employees and employees of government contractors receive the same rights and protections afforded private sector workers. These and other executive orders can be searched at this site.

MANAGEMENT CONSULTANTS

Global Human Resource Sevices Ltd.

http://www.globalhr.com

Provides policy design, management, host-country support, cross-cultural training, destination, and other support services.

Hunter Group
http://www.hunter-group.com

Specialists in financial and human resource information management systems consulting.

Impact Consulting Group
http://www.impactconsultinggroup.com

Academic and practice-based human resource management products and services.

Management Advantage
http://www.garlic.com/tma

A human resource management consulting and training web site.

Management Consulting Online
http://www.cob.ohio-state.edu/~fin/jobs/mco/mco.html

Covers careers, thought, trends, and firms in the field of management consulting.

Online Career Center
http://www.occ.com

This site provides information on downsizing and the use of outplacement services to help employees reestablish career goals and secure new employment. Includes advice on working with outplacement services and what to expect from professional counselors.

Personnel Office
http://www.personneloffice.com

Personnel Office specializes in helping small businesses manage human resource objectives while working with federal and state employment regulations. Their services include employment consulting, employee handbooks, job descriptions, performance management, terminations and more.

Personnel Systems Associates
http://users.aol.com/mding/who.html

A human resources management consulting firm, PSA specializes in employee compensation, training, performance appraisal, personnel computer systems, and expert witness testimony.

Watson Wyatt Worldwide
http://www.watsonwyatt.com

Watson Wyatt Worldwide is one of the world's leading human resources and risk management consulting firms, with 5,000 associates in 89 offices around the world. They help organizations of all types and sizes make their business strategies work, through innovative programs that develop, motivate and empower employees.

Winning Associates
http://www.all-biz.com/winning

This management consulting firm offers over 200 articles on a variety of topics online.

MEDIATION AND DISPUTE RESOLUTION

Alternative Dispute Resolution
http://www.adr.org/guide.html

Does your organization use alternatives to litigation for resolving disputes? This site will help you explore arbitration and mediation options.

American Arbitration Association of Dispute Resolution Services
http://www.adr.org

Includes rules and procedures, guides, ethics and standards, articles and press releases on labor, employment, insurance, corporate and commercial issues.

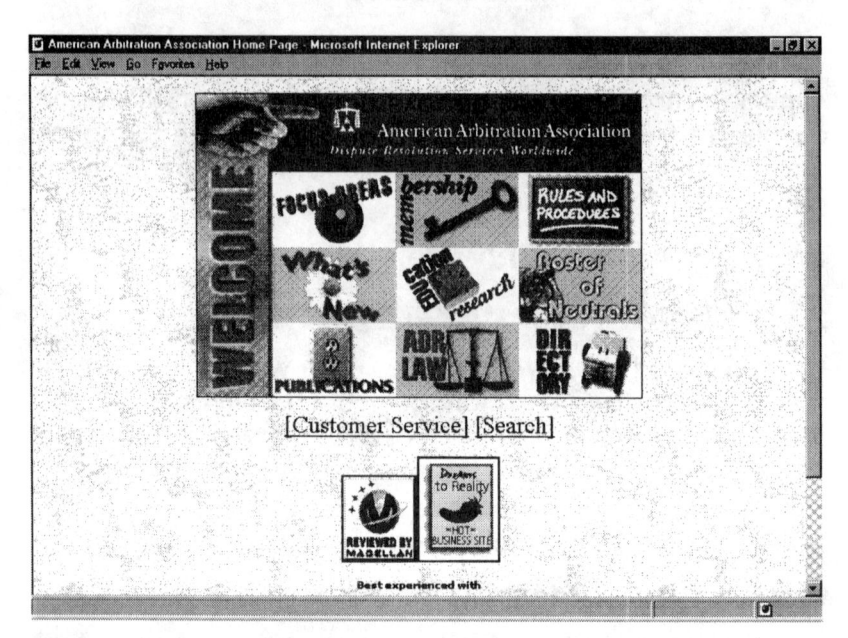

Caras & Associates, Inc.
> http://www.carasadr.com

Information on alternative dispute resolution, an increasingly popular alternative for resolving employer/employee disputes.

Dispute Resolution and Conflict Avoidance for the Construction Industry
> http://www.ramco-ins.com/webl.htm

Encourages partnering to avoid disputes in the construction industry. Sponsored by the American Arbitration Association.

Liszt Email Discussion Group Directory
> http://www.liszt.com

This Web site includes conflict resolution and industrial relations listservs, newsgroups, and bulletin boards.

National Labor Relations Board
http://wwwr.nlrb.gov

Information on the laws governing relations between labor unions and employers involved in interstate commerce.

Vincent Boudreau and Associates
http://www.netour.com/vincent.htm

Consulting firm specializing in conflict resolution, collective bargaining, and labor relations.

OTHER RESOURCES

CNN.FN
http://www.cnnfn.com/mybusiness/9601/29/mentors/

This site describes the effect that a mentoring program can have on productivity in your organization.

Cornell University Center for Advanced Human Resource Studies
http://www.ilr.cornell.edu/depts/cahrs

Partnership between faculty and 50 major corporations conducts human resource management research.

Dilbert Zone
http://www.unitedmedia.com/comics/dilbert

Scott Adams' popular interpretations of office situations can be useful for training and employee communications.

G-Neil Companies
http://www.gneil.com

G-Neil offers time and money-saving human resources solutions for business professionals worldwide. They have over 1,500 HR products to choose from.

HR Manager

http://www.auxillium.com/contents.htm

This site bills itself as "the first comprehensive human resources guide written in hypertext." Includes information on effective organizations, staffing issues, compensation and benefits policies, and record-keeping requirements. It also contains a glossary of federal employment statutes affecting employees.

HR Online, The Human Resources Mall

http://www.hr2000.com

Human resources services, products, software and discussion groups.

HR Power Guide

http://www.cam.org/steinbg/hurepg.htm

Provides descriptions of over 200 safety and health, security, and staffing products.

Human Resource Development Press

http://www.hrdpress.com

Print, video, and electronic resources are described here.

Human Resources Headquarters

http://www.hrhq.com

Provides information on the latest solutions and trends for human resource managers.

Human Resources Institute

http://hri.eckerd.edu/about.html

HRI tracks more than 100 people-management issues and produces lengthy reports which only members may download. But anyone who clicks on "guest login" can read about the issue of the month, search the complete report library by keyword, and retrieve detailed tables of contents that amount to an overview of the forces driving each issue. Nonmembers can also use the "Internet information sources" page, which presents hundreds of nicely annotated human resource links in numerous categories.

Human Resources Management Systems

http://htnews.idirect.com/hrnews/get/ hrmanagementsystems.html

This is a human resources management systems newsgroup. You can use this site to discuss your concerns and questions relating to issues surrounding HR management systems, or simply to discuss HR issues with other HR professionals.

Human Resources Plaza Reading Room

http://www.hodes.com/hr_plaza/ hr_02.html

New publications are added each month.

Internet Service Providers

http://thelist.iworld.com

There are over 5,165 Internet Service Providers listed here. You can search by name, by state, by area code, or graphic map.

Office of the American Workplace

http://www.fed.org/uscompanies/labor

Profiles of companies illustrating effective use of best practices.

Peer Resources Homepage

http://www.islandnet.com/~rcarr/ peer.html

Information on peer helping and peer support in corporations.

Personnel Concepts

http://www.pclimited.com

Personnel Concepts offers over 200 human resource and safety products, including state/Federal labor law posters.

Small Business Administration

http://www.sbaonline.sba.gov

Gopher searches, downloadable files, and other resources are available from this federal government agency.

Techweb

http://techweb.com

This is an excellent site for human resource professionals who need to be updated on the latest products in the technology field. It includes *Techwire* magazine, with many articles on the latest developments in the technology field.

Up-to-Date Library

http://www.utdlibrary.com

The Up-to-Date Library human resource management division provides unlimited access to over 6,000 articles from 1994 to the current month, immediate article reprints by fax or mail, monthly list of the "hot" topics in HR management.

Workforce Online

http://www.workforceonline.com

This is the *Workforce* magazine Web site. It contains searchable access to many magazine articles and has a conference room where human resource experts can share ideas.

OUTPLACEMENT

Lee Hecht Harrison

http://www.careerlhh.com

Outplacement, career, and redeployment services. Site includes outplacement tools and an executive talent directory.

Online Career Center

http://www.occ.com/occ/NBEW/OutplacementConsultant.html

This site provides information on downsizing and the use of outplacement services to help employees reestablish career goals and secure new employment. Includes advice on working with outplacement services and what to expect from professional counselors.

Human Resource Store

http://www.hrstore.com

Provides training tools and outsourcing options for training, recruiting and outplacement services.

PAYROLL

Automatic Data Processing

http://www.adp.com/index.html

One of the world's largest independent computing services companies, handling payroll for over 350,000 clients.

HRM-One

http://www.harmony-solutions.com.au

HRM-One is a developer of human resource management and payroll systems software.

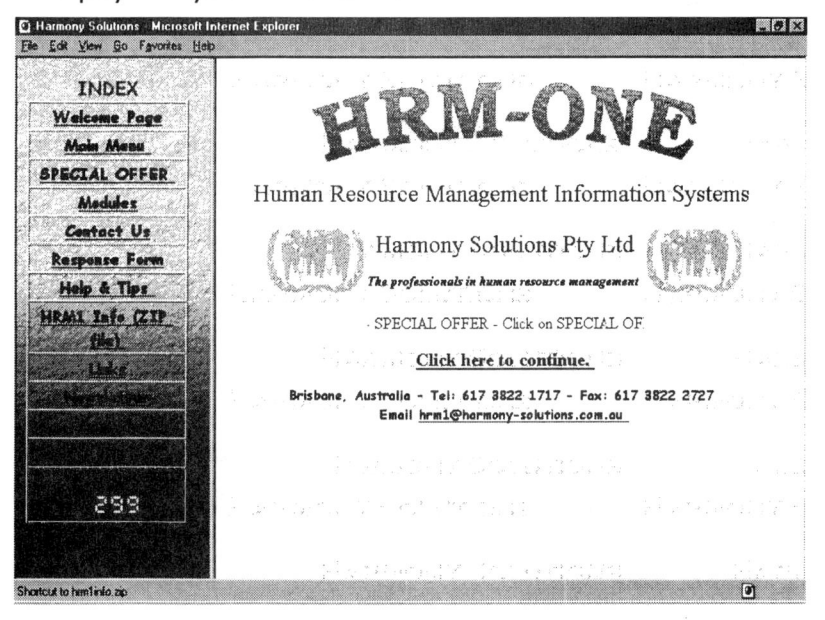

ICONtrol, Inc.
http://www.icontrol.net

The new ICONtrol human resources payroll system, integrated with Great Plains Dynamics Payroll, allows single data entry to provide instant, real-time access to both HR and payroll information in one, saving time and money, and eliminating costly errors.

Payroll Legal Alert
http://www.ahipubs.com

This newsletter will give you expert advice in complying with new laws and regulations that dramatically impact payroll management, including tax changes from the IRS, legislation from Congress, and rulings from the Department of Labor.

Time+Plus
http://www.timekeeping-payroll.com

This site describes a software program featuring an automated electronic timekeeping and payroll service.

QUALITY

American Productivity and Quality Center
http://www.apqc.org

A non-profit organization dedicated to helping companies find and adopt best practices.

American Society for Quality Control
http://www.asqc.org

Presents information on process improvement, teamwork, and quality standards.

International Organization for Standardization
http://www.iso.ch/welcome.html

Information on the International Organization for Standardization, including the ISO 9000 News Service.

RECRUITMENT

All Business Network
http://www.all-biz.com/articles/jd.htm

This site covers how to conduct a job analysis and write a proper job description. Includes examples of job descriptions and the uses of job descriptions

America's Job Bank
http://www.ajb.dni.us

Post job openings online.

American Association of Colleges and Employers
http://www.jobweb.org

Helps thousands of college career services professionals and human resource professionals in the service and manufacturing sectors network, matching college graduates with potential employers.

Bernard Hodes Advertising
http://www.hodes.com

Put the resources of one of the world's leading recruitment advertising agencies to work on your recruiting program. Bernard Hodes Advertising, home of CareerMosaic, offers award-winning talent and service in offices worldwide.

Career Mosaic
http://www.careermosaic.com

Lists job openings.

Careerpath
http://www.careerpath.com

This site presents employment ads from many major newspapers: *Washington Post, Boston Globe, Chicago Tribune, Denver Post, Los Angeles Times, Miami Herald, New York Times, Orlando Sentinel, Philadelphia Inquirer* and many more. Leading newspapers across the nation have joined to create the World Wide Web's most complete employment database.

Anyone with access to the Internet can search through a broad spectrum of jobs from entry level to executive. Careerpath is easy to use, updated daily and is free to job hunters. More than 250,000 new jobs are added each month.

Career Web

http://www.cweb.com

Advertising for high tech jobs.

Electronic Recruiting News

http://www.interbiznet.com/ern

A daily online newsletter for recruiters, placement firms and human resource managers.

Greentree Systems

http://www.greentreesystems.com

Software solutions for managing the recruitment process.

Heart Advertising Network

http://www.career.com

An interactive recruitment advertising site.

IBN

http://www.interbiznet.com/ern

Electronic recruiting news targeted directly at human resource professionals is presented at this site.

Janweb

http://janweb.icdi.wvu.edu/kinder

Learn how many companies are modifying their recruitment and selection processes in order to comply with the Americans with Disabilities Act. Provides examples of areas affected by the ADA.

JobSmart

http://www.jobsmart.com

Search over 50,000 resumes online.

JobWeb

http://www.jobweb.org

Job listings and resumes. Sponsored by the National Association of Colleges and Employers.

Kelly Services

http://www.kellyservices.com

Leader in providing staffing and related services.

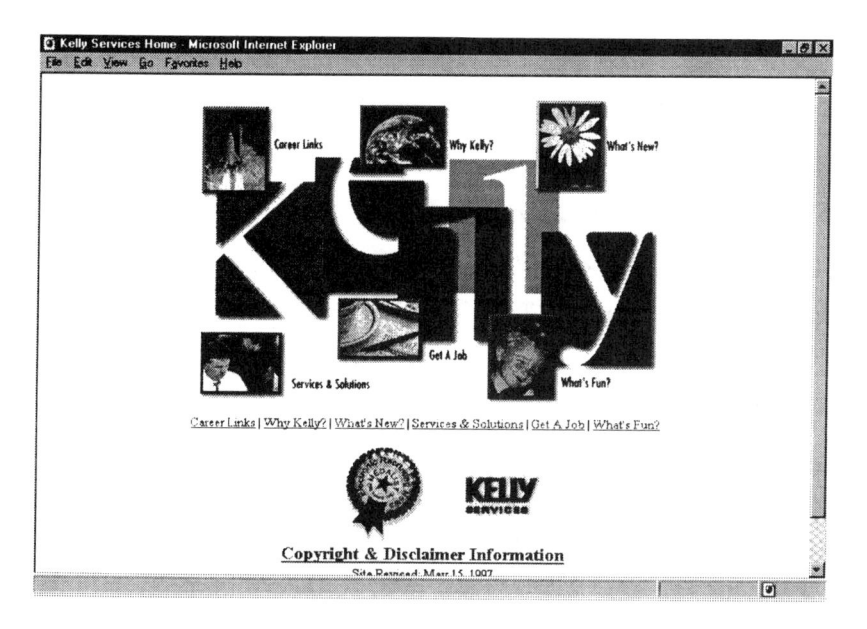

Lee Hecht Harrison

http://www.careerlhh.com

Outplacement, career development and redeployment services and research data. Site includes outplacement tools and an executive talent directory.

Management Recruiters International
http://www.mrinet.com

MRI, one of the world's largest search and recruitment firms, finds the best executive, managerial, professional, and technical talent for their clients. The worldwide MRI network helps client companies meet staffing challenges, such as permanent outplacement, flexible staffing, videoconferencing, and relocation through outsourcing and retainers.

Manpower
http://www.manpower.com

One of the world's largest staffing services for office, industrial, and technical professionals.

Monster Board
http://www.monster.com

Post job openings and search over 70,000 resumés.

Nationwide Advertising Service
http://www.hrads.com

Provides information on placement services, research reports, workforce diversity, and employee communications products.

NetStart
http://www.careerbuilder.com

NetStart, Inc. offers a Web-based recruiting solution that gives human resource professionals the ability to manage all the processes involved in Internet recruiting, including creating Web pages detailing job openings and company information and managing electronic responses generated from the Internet. NetStart's solutions include CareerBuilder, a career search Web site for job seekers. The company is also partnering with two career search sites, the Monster Board and Career Mosaic, to extend its Internet recruiting reach.

TeamBuilder is a turnkey recruiting application for the Web designed for HR professionals. It was designed to model recruiting workflow processes, including posting job openings, receiving, reviewing and routing resumés on-line, searching for resumes, replying to candidates via e-mail, and measuring results of recruiting programs.

Using TeamBuilder's Job-Posting Wizard, human resource professionals can build Web pages for each job offering with no HTML programming. The HR executive enters the job information into a series of templates to build and change job postings.

Office Mates 5 from MRI
http://mrinet.com/om5

MRI specializes in finding the best in office support staff. From secretarial and clerical to accounting support and data processing talent, they can determine the skill level and track record of each candidate and refer those most qualified for your specific requirements.

Olsten Staffing Services
http://www.olsten.com

Infomation on Olsten's services and flexible staffing solutions, including traditional temporary help, specialty staffing, strategic partnerships, and outsourcing.

Online Career Center
http://www.occ.com

Place employment ads and review resumés at this site.

Recruiters OnLine Network
http://www.ipa.com

The Recruiters OnLine Network is composed of employment firms worldwide. With over 3,500 participating companies, they are the largest online association of recruiters, search firms, employment agencies and employment professionals.

Recruitment and Training Administration
http://www.doleta.gov/programs/onet/

The Occupational Information Network is a comprehensive database that describes occupations, job skills, and requirements for a wide variety of positions in all sectors of the economy.

Restrac Inc.
http://www.restrac.com

Staffing simulation software providers offer information on their products.

Simply Better
http://www.esc.ttnc.doleta.gov/simplyb

A network of employment and training organizations and professionals committed to improving their services and customer satisfaction through continuous improvement.

Software Technology Corp.
http://www.headhunter.net

Software Technology Corp. has developed a free, full-featured recruiting application which posts job opportunities and resumes on the World Wide Web. Headhunter.net provides employment seekers with unlimited, free access to job listings and allows recruiters to post their listings at no charge.

Headhunter.net also provides geographical job searches, key word searches, immediate job postings, continuous database updates, and protection of private recruiting information. Recruiters can search for job candidates by background and by location, as well as write and post detailed job listings directly on the service and instantly update salary or other criteria as needed.

Techweb
http://www.techweb.com/careers/careers.html

Tech careers lets you post jobs to this massive database. Job listings will stay active for eight weeks. It is accessible on all of the four commercial online services: American On-Line,

CompuServe, Prodigy and Microsoft Network. There are more than 10,000 jobs listed.

US Group—Intersourcing Online

http://www.usgroup.org

Resources on intersourcing are provided at this site.

Virtual Job Fair

http://www.vjf.com

A site for recruiters seeking high tech professionals.

RELOCATION

Employee Relocation Council

http://www.erc.org/research/tips.htm

Relocation information for new employees moving from another state, including moving checklists and hints for children.

Relocation Journal

http://www.relojournal.com

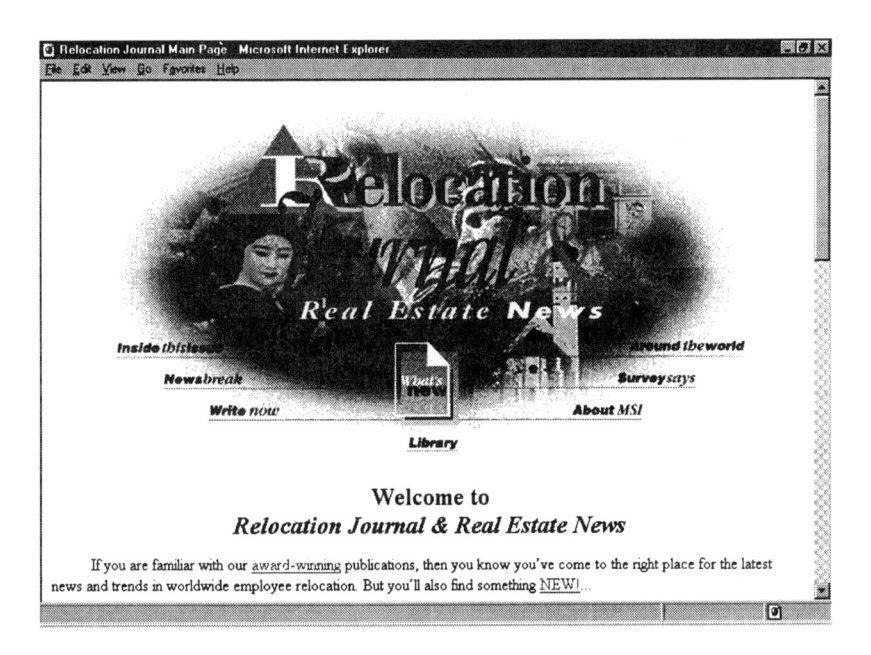

This site includes links to resources about relocation destinations in the United States and around the world, as well as a weekly newsletter and highlights from the flagship monthly publication.

Relocation Resources
> http://www.rriworld.com

Information on US and overseas relocation services.

Runzheimer International
> http://www.runzheimer.com

Relocation administration services.

Salary Calculator
> http://www.homefair.com/

Use this tool to compare the cost of living in hundreds of cities in the US and abroad. This is especially valuable when dealing with employee relocation.

Salary Information/Salary Survey Sites
> http://www.hodes.com/hr_plaza/hr_11.html

Site provides a relocation salary calculator and salary information by profession.

SAFETY

Agency for Toxic Substances and Disease Registry
> http://www.atsdr1.cdc.gov:8080/atsdrhome.html

Provides a complete listing of all toxic checmicals.

American Federation of State, County and Municipal Employees
> http://www.afscme.org

Information on workplace safety and health issues, workplace violence, disabilities, and AIDS.

American National Standards Institute
http://www.ansi.org/home.html

ANSI is the source of standards in a wide range of safety topics, many of which were adopted by the US when OSHA was established.

American Society for Industrial Security
http://www.asisonline.org

The latest developments in security practice and technology.

Centers for Disease Control
http://www.cdc.gov

Medical information and health statistics from the CDC.

Denison University Campus Security and Safety
http://www.denison.edu/sec-safe/

Site includes employee safety training, laboratory safety, and government mandated safety plans.

Duke University Occupational and Environmental Medicine
http://occ-env-med.mc.duke.edu/oem

Contains information on a wide array of occupational and environmenal health topics, as well as many OSHA, NIOSH and EPA documents.

Emergency Preparedness Information Exchange
gopher://hoshi.cic.sfu.ca

Promotes disaster mitigation research and practice through information on emergency and disaster management organizations, topics, conferences, and other emergency management resources.

Environmental Protection Agency
http://www.epa.gov

Site provides information on regulations affecting employers and employees, compliance issues, and available publications.

Environmental Resource Center

http://www.ftp.clearlake.ibm.com/erc/homepage.html

Provides a range of environmental data.

Federal Emergency Management Agency

http://www.fema.gov

Information on hazards threatening communities, personal protection measures to take in a disaster, and information on the Disaster Unemployment Insurance program.

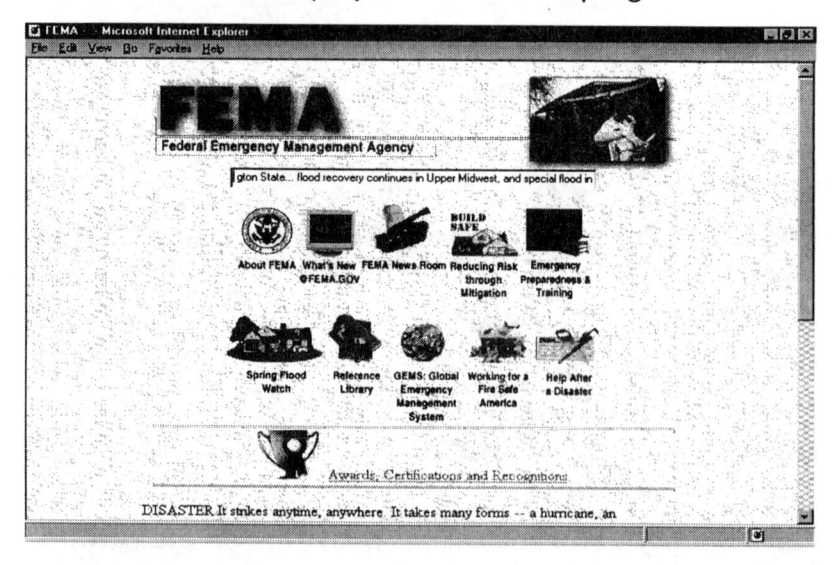

Federal Register

http://www.access.gpo.gov/su_docs/aces/aacess001.html

Features documents from the Federal Register and instructions on accessing the daily Federal Register on the Internet.

FedWorld

http://www.fedworld.gov

Scientific, technical, and other information provided through the National Technical Information Service.

Government Institutes

http://www.govinst.com

Books, software and courses on a wide variety of environmental and occupational safety and health topics.

MSDS Online

gopher://atlas.chem.utah.edu:70/11/MSDS

MSDS sheets arranged alphabetically by chemical name.

National Council on Compensation Insurance

http://www.ncci.com/index.html

Includes information on conducting a job safety analysis, workers' compensation claim characteristics, and classification data.

National Institute of Occupational Safety and Health

http://www.cdc.gov/niosh/homepage.html

The federal agency which conducts safety and industrial hygiene research presents lists of publications and videos available, as well as fact sheets on indoor air quality, back belts, and carpal tunnel syndrome.

National Safety Council

http://www.nsc.org

Information and resources on workplace, environmental, traffic, and home safety.

Occupational Safety and Health Administration

http://www.osha.gov

Use OSHA's web page to keep up on the latest developments in workplace safety. Includes press releases, publications, frequently asked questions, and more.

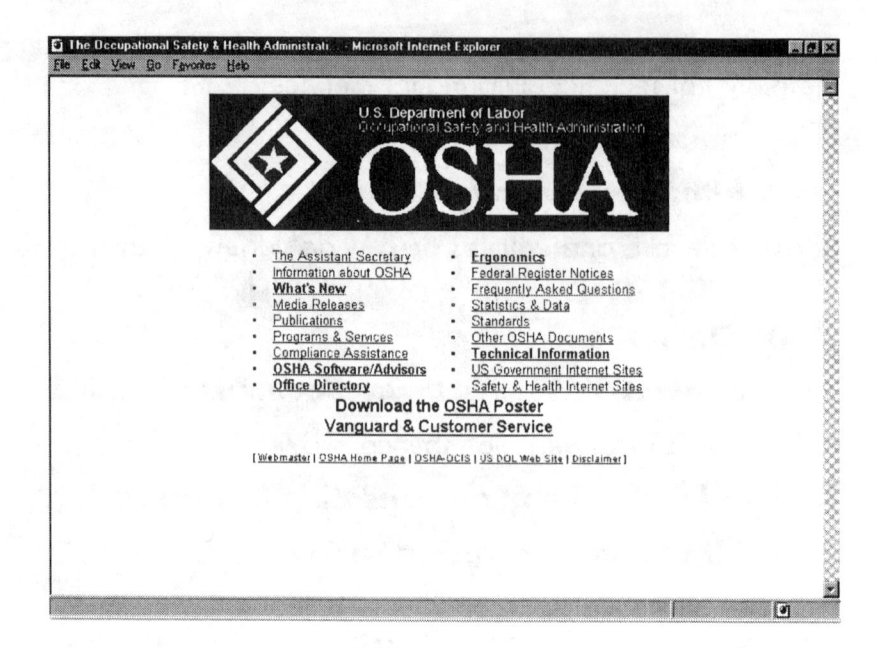

Safety Pays

> http://www.safetypays.com

Safety Pays is a low cost employee incentive program designed to reduce workers compensation claims in virtually any business. This motivational program averages a 50% reduction in a company's losses in the first year of use. It features an exciting, innovative approach, which generates both employee enthusiasm and commitment to preventing on-the-job accidents. Safety Pays can be expanded to include human resources issues such as absenteeism and tardiness.

US Department of Energy

> http://www.tis.eh.doe.gov/tis.html

DOE's environment safety and health technical information services provides information on safety and health issues.

SECURITY

American Society for Industrial Security

> http://www.asisonline.org

Organization of security professionals presents latest developments in security practice and technology for development and management of security programs.

SELECTION

Alexander Information Group
http://www.mhv.net/~alexinfogp

A background check service providing public record information on job applicants. Also offers pre-employment screening software.

All Business Network
http://www.all-biz.com/quests.html

Interviewing techniques, including what questions can and cannot be asked legally.

Application Profiles
http://www.ap-profiles.com

Application Profiles is a national information retrieval and verification company providing comprehensive services to employers. Their primary focus is on employment-related background checks. They can design a customized screening program consistent with your organization's goals.

Assessment Systems Inc.
http://www.asisolutions.com

Information on selection, assessment, hiring and development of outstanding employees.

CIC Applicant Background Checks
http://www.backtrak.com

Software manages and automates the background checking process. A variety of types of searches and a demonstration are available.

Court TV

http://www.courttv.com/seminars/handbook

Information on preparing reference check policies.

Employment Testing and Screening

http://www.employment-test.com

This site provides computerized employment screening services and features the Personality Plus employment testing system.

HR Plus

http://www.hrplus.com

This company produces pre-employment background reports using professional reference interviews, criminal history, driving records, education verification, drug testing, credit history, and workers compensation information.

Informus Employment Screening

http://www.informus.com

Nationwide pre-employment screening service.

Integrity Center
http://www.integctr.com

Services include education and employment verification, personal credit and driver license history checks, and drug testing.

Keirsey Temperament Sorter—Jungian Personality Test
http://sunsite.unc.edu/jembin/mb.pl

Site covers a personality test and summary of personality typing.

Online Journal of Ethics
http://condor.depaul.edu/ethics/hand.html

Article on how handwriting analysis can be used in pre-employment screening to reveal important character traits.

Rio Communications
http://www.rio.com/~tstmastr/amenu.html

Basic information on using psychological testing for job applicant screening.

SEXUAL HARRASSMENT

American Psychological Association
http://www.apa.org/pubinfo/harass.html

Facts and myths about sexual harrassment are presented here to increase human resource professionals ability to deal with these issues.

Harassment Hotline
http://www.end-harassment.com

This site was created for employers because all employers are required to provide an effective system for reporting sexual harassment in the workplace. This system provides employers with conclusive evidence to combat or end sexual harassment. Many good tips for employers can be found at this Web site.

Interactive Employment Training
http://www.hrtrain.com

Company offers interactive sexual harrassment training on CD-ROM.

Training Source
http://www.rctm.com

The Training Source is a full service resource for video and computer-based training materials, including sexual harassment topics.

Women Against Sexual Harassment
http://www.pic.net/w-a-s-h

WASH is a non-profit corporation formed to assist victims of sexual harassment who do not know where to go for help. This is a site with practical advice from people who have experienced sexual harassment in the workplace.

SMOKING

University of California/Berkeley
http://server.berkeley.edu/DailyCal/Issues/09.27.95/smoking.txt

Article discusses risks of second-hand smoke and how to manage the conflicts between smokers and non-smokers in the work environment.

SOFTWARE/TECHNOLOGY

Access Corporation
http://www.recruitsuite.com/internet.html

Markets Recruit Suite features applicant tracking and recruiting software, and a full range of resume scanning and Internet/Intranet applications.

Advanced Personnel Systems
http://www.hrcensus.com

This site has a complete listing of sources of human resource management software and computer based training courseware. Some of the types of software offered include employee testing, training administration, performance management, career development, skills management, and human resource planning software. Information on HR vendors, products and consultants is also provided.

Again Technologies
http://www.againtech.com

This site provides information on software and consulting to help administer profit sharing, sales commission, executive compensation, and incentive compensation plans.

Application Group
http://www.appgroup.com

This site offers integrated solutions in the areas of human resources and finance, specializing in strategic planning, reengineering, systems integration and software.

Austin-Hayne Corp.
http://www.austin-hayne.com

Provides software tools to improve employee performance and productivity.

Automatic Data Processing
http://www.adp.com/index.html

One of the world's largest independent computing services companies, handling payroll for over 350,000 clients.

Benefit Software, Inc.
http://www.bsiweb.com

BSI is a leading developer of highly specialized employee fringe benefits, communications and workers compensation case management software systems. *Fringe Facts* is an employee benefit software system that produces personalized fringe benefit statements for employers. *Comp Watch* is a workers compensation case management and claims tracking system that produces the employer's injury and illness form.

Berkshire Associates

http://www.berkshire-aap.com

Software program supports affirmative action programs, handling statistical reports and data.

Best Software (ABRA Systems)

http://www.bestsoftware.com/_frames/ about.frameset.html

Software designed to help human resources and payroll departments manage employee information, recruitment, payroll processing, and regulatory compliance.

Centra Software

http://www.centra.com

Offers an online demonstration of distance education software.

CIC Applicant Background Checks

http://www.backtrak.com

Software manages and automates the background checking process. A variety of types of searches and a demonstration are available.

Clayton Wallis Co.

http://www.crl.com/~clwallis

Samples of software for compensation planning and salary structure modeling.

Consultant Team Inc.

http://www.intimesystems.com

Client/server and mainframe human resources and payroll systems are discussed at this site.

Criterion Inc.
http://www.criterioninc.com

Software for managing affirmative action plans, succession and career planning, and training.

Cybernetics
http://www.cybernetics.com

This site provides an overview of Cybernetics' workforce management software products and links to the Web sites of other companies. The site offers visitors a free Workforce Calculator, a tool that allows visitors to test drive a portion of the planning and budgeting functions automated by Cybernetics' Workforce Manager software. The software helps call centers employ the right number of people to handle calls without compromising service. Other call center management programs are also available.

Cyborg Systems Inc.
http://www.cyborg.com

Human resources, payroll processing, and benefits administration software.

Edify—Electronic Workforce
http://www.edify.com

Software enables organizations to provide automated services over the Internet, intranets, e-mail, and by phone.

Genelco Inc.
http://www.genelco.com

Software and outsourcing for group health and pension administration.

Genesys Systems Software
http://www.genesys-soft.com

Provider of software solutions for managing human resource information.

Griggs Productions, Inc.
http://www.griggs.com

No Potential Lost is a software program that clarifies of how diversity, relationship and cultural dynamics affect performance in the workplace. You can increase productivity, creativity and innovation while preventing costly losses at all levels. With compelling content and multi-media technology, this series ensures effective learning. Free demo disk available.

HR and Compensation Systems Census
http://www.hrcensus.com

Objective information on software available to help human resources professionals manage personnel, compensation, and benefits issues.

HR Press Software
http://www.hrpress-software.com

A human resource software and computer-based training library, featuring over 150 software programs for every conceivable HR task.

Human Resource MicroSystems
http://www.hrms.com

Human resource tracking and employee self-service via corporate intranets.

Humanic Design
http://www.humanic.com

Company provides human resource management software and related services.

Hunter Group
http://www.hunter-group.com

Firm specializes in using client/server software to redesign and improve human resource processes.

Information Learning Systems
http://www.planexpert.com

Software provides scripted answers to employee and retiree questions about benefits, payroll and human resource policies.

International Association for Human Resource Information Management
http://www.IHRMIM.org

Information on vendors of human resource management software.

InTime Solutions
http://www.intimesoft.com

Shift, post and location assignment software cuts operating costs and improves morale.

KPMG
http://www.kpmg.com

Get the next generation of software for managing global assignments. It's comprehensive, flexible, easy to learn, easy to customize, easy to use, runs in a Windows environment and is supported by KPMG International Services. Learn how KPMG/LINK connects employers to their global workforces.

Lawson Software
http://www.lawson.com

Integrated human resource, finance, and procurement software. Many HR professionals have to deal with form distribution, redundant data entry and legal documentation which can consume as much as 60% of a human resource department's time. Lawson Insight's human resource, payroll and benefits system eliminates unnecessary paperwork, cuts costs, and enables employees to perform a full spectrum of activities from their desktop.

Logical Design Solutions
http://www.lds.com

LDS creates highly interactive, self-service human resources solutions using the latest web platforms, intranet, Internet and extranet technology. The LDS team includes software architects, designers, performance engineers, business analysts and developers. They try to understand your needs and how to make your HR functions more efficient.

NetStart
http://www.careerbuilder.com

NetStart, Inc. offers a Web-based recruiting solution that gives human resource professionals the ability to manage all the processes involved in Internet recruiting, including creating Web pages detailing job openings and company information and managing electronic responses generated from the Internet. NetStart's solutions include CareerBuilder, a career search Website for job seekers. The company is also partnering with two career search sites, the Monster Board and Career Mosaic, to extend its Internet recruiting reach.

TeamBuilder is a turnkey recruiting application for the Web designed for HR professionals. It was designed to model recruiting workflow processes, including posting job openings, receiving, reviewing and routing resumes on-line, searching for resumes, replying to candidates via e-mail, and measuring results of recruiting programs.

Using TeamBuilder's Job-Posting Wizard, human resource professionals can build Web pages for each job offering with no HTML programming. The HR executive enters the job information into a series of templates to build and change job postings.

PayAmerica
http://www.payamerica.com

PayAmerica is a Windows-based software package for payroll and human resource functions.

Presenting Solutions, Inc.
http://www.presol.com

PSI is a computer-based testing and training service offering challenging skills evaluation systems for pre/post training and pre-employment assessment. It provides the temporary staffing industry and corporate human resource departments with software skills evaluation systems for popular PC/Windows and Macintosh platform business software applications.

PRI Associates
http://www.priassoc.com

State of the art affirmative action planning and skills assessment software solutions.

Questar Corp.
http://www.questarcorp.com/compstar

Customizable employee appraisal software stores employee information, managers' and personnel department comments.

Resumix
http://www.resumix.com/index.html

Expert systems technology for staffing automation.

Ross Systems InfoCentral
http://www.rossinc.com

Software applications for staffing, benefits administration, employee development, payroll, and health and safety.

SAP America
http://www.sap-ag.de

Provider of global client/server business software applications.

Sierra Systems Consultants
http://www.sierrasys.com

Software consultants to the human resources profession for over 20 years.

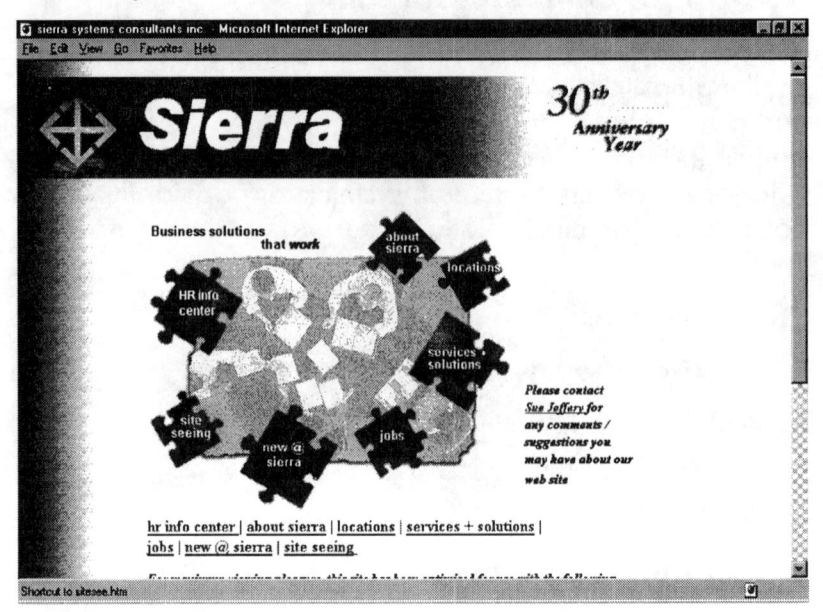

Software Plus

> http://www.softwareplus.com

Human resource information system products, services and support are offered.

Software Technology Corp.

> http://www.headhunter.net

Software Technology Corp. has developed a free, full-featured recruiting application which posts job opportunities and resumés on the World Wide Web. Headhunter.net provides employment seekers with unlimited, free access to job listings and allows recruiters to post their listings at no charge.

Headhunter.net also provides geographical job searches, key word searches, immediate job postings, continuous database updates, and protection of private recruiting information. Recruiters can search for job candidates by background and by location as well as write and post detailed job listings directly on the service and instantly update salary or other criteria as needed.

Spectrum Human Resource Systems Corp.
http://www.spectrumhr.com

Human resource information systems and training administration software are described.

StarGarden Quality Human Resources and Payroll Software
http://www.stargarden.com

Information on employee demographics, recruiting and applicant tracking, training and development, health and safety, and labor relations software.

Strategic Management Group Inc.
http://www.smginc.com

Business training trends and software solutions are presented.

Target Vision
http://www.targetvision.com

Information on online employee communications options.

TECo Enterprises Inc.
http://www.tecoinc.com

Provides an overview of computer-based testing systems, featuring test authoring, administration, and reporting.

Time+Plus
http://www.timekeeping-payroll.com

This site describes a software program featuring an automated electronic timekeeping and payroll service.

TimeVision Inc.
http://www.timevision.com

The software presented on this site can build organizational charts from human resource data.

Ultimate Software Group
http://www.usgroup.com

Developer of human resource management systems for medium-size businesses offers product details and news of relevant legislative changes.

VideoFax Systems
http://www.videofax.com

Desktop broadcasting software simplifies employee communications via multimedia.

William Steinberg Consultants, Inc.
http://www.cam.org/steinbg

Producers of software products for human resource management and the *HR Power Guide*, a catalog of HR software. Award winning *EASY GEN* software makes it easy to create, conduct and analyze employee surveys. The Windows version includes hundreds of sample questions, support for numerous question types, custom answer scales, fast data collection, colorful, ans customizable graphs. Download a free, fully working demo from this Website.

Work Wise—Desktop and Intranet Solutions
http://www.workwise.com

View a sample of *HR Web Builder*, a software program for managing employee information.

Xalta Interactive
http://www.xalta.com

Survey software allows organizations to survey employees across intranets or the Internet.

STATISTICS

Bureau of Economic Analysis
http://www.bea.doc.gov

Information on economic growth, regional development, and the nation's position in the world economy.

Bureau of Labor Statistics
http://stats.bls.gov:80/datahome.htm
http://stats.bls.gov/intcat2.htm

This site provides a wide variety of reports and news releases, including economic, employment, and workplace injury and illness data. Links to other Federal and international statistical agencies are provided, including the Census Bureau, Bureau of Economic Analysis, Economic Research Service, and National Center for Health Statistics. Information on seminars on collecting and analyzing data and applying results to human resource policy development is also available.

Demographic Data Viewer
http://sedac.ciesin.org/plue/ddviewer

Provides rapid data mapping, viewing and analysis.

Government Information Locator Service
http://www.access.gpo.gov/su_docs/gils/gils.html

A resource for finding Federal information online.

LMI NET—ALMIS Home Page
http://ecuvax.cis.ecu.edu/~lmi/lmi.html

A comprehensive labor market information system featuring links to Federal and state resources.

Office of Economic Cooperation and Development
http://www.oecd.org/std

Monthly updates of international labor, economic, and demographic information are provided, including tables and graphs.

Salary Information/Salary Survey Sites

http://www.hodes.com/hr_plaza/hr_11.html

Site provides salary information by profession and a relocation salary calculator.

SAS Institute

http://www.sas.com

Provider of enterprise data management software for decisionmaking in business, industry, education, and government.

SPSS

http://www.spss.com

SPSS provides statistical product and service solutions for surveys, quality improvement, education, and government reporting.

Statistics Canada

http://www.statcan.ca.start.html

Health, income, labor, and cultural data, research papers, and news are offered.

STAT-USA

http://www.stat-usa.gov

Business and economic information compiled by the US Department of Commerce from over 50 Federal agencies.

TAXES

Cyber Accountant

http://www.cyber-cpa.com

The Cyber Accountant provides answers to tax, financial and accounting questions and helps users find accountants, CPA, enrolled agents, financial planners, or other financial professionals.

Internal Revenue Service

http://www.irs.ustreas.gov/plain

The IRS home page provides access to authoritative federal tax information and forms.

TELECOMMUTING

Gil Gordon Associates

http://www.gilgordon.com/

If you are considering telecommuting, telework, and alternative officing, this is a valuable site to visit. It presents clear, thorough and practical information focusing on linking people and documents wherever they can be found. Interested in the two volumes on telework just published in Bonn? A link takes you to the German publisher's site. Annotated links to federal, state, local, regional, and rural agencies and projects, associations, vendors, and articles.

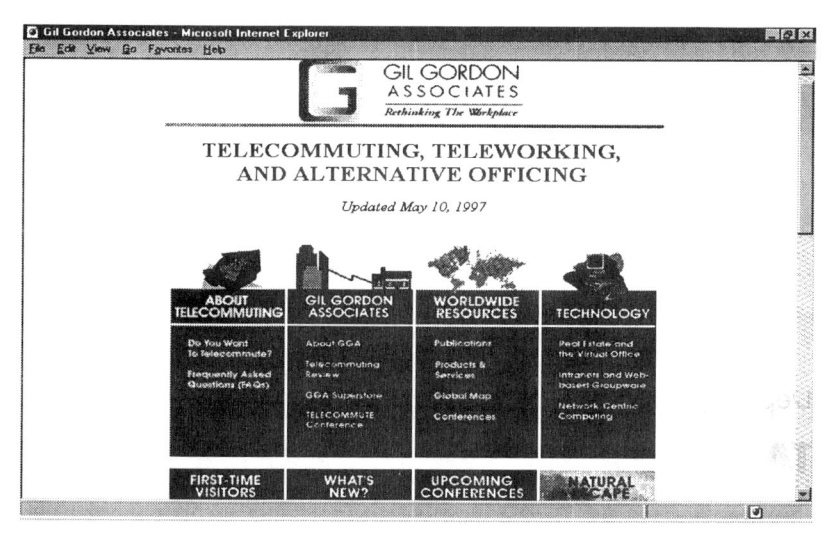

Pacific Bell

http://www.pacbell.com/Lib/TCGuide/tc-10.html

The basics of telecommuting, reasons for implementing a telecommuting program, management tips, and the technological considerations of working at home and at satellite offices.

Technology, HR & Communication Home Page
http://www.inforamp.net/~bcroft

Information on new and emerging technologies for communications.

TEMPORARY AND ALTERNATIVE STAFFING

Accountemps
http://www.accountemps.com

Accountemps is the leader in temporary financial staffing with offices throughout the United States, Canada and Europe. They provide the highest-quality financial specialists including bookkeepers, CPAs and controllers. In a recent national survey, Accountemps was rated as having the most qualified financial temporaries.

Adminstaff
http://www.administaff.com

This firm offers human resource departments administrative and secretarial support services.

Armor Personnel
http://www.inforamp.net/~armor

Armor is a professional outsourcing firm providing flexible staffing, employee leasing, recruiting, and employee development.

Certified Systems, Inc.
http://www.leasedemployees.com

CSI offers a permanent staffing solution to small and medium size companies experiencing hardships due to increasing governmental regulations and rising workers compensation and health care costs, while providing all of the benefits and protection of statutory workers compensation insurance. CSI provides services in the areas of risk management, human resources, payroll management, and employee benefits programs.

Management Recruiters International
http://www.mrinet.com

The worldwide MRI network helps client companies meet staffing challenges, including flexible staffing.

National Association of Temporary and Staffing Services
http://www.natss.org

NATSS was founded as the Institute of Temporary Services to ensure that competent temporary help services were available to business and industry, while simultaneously providing flexible employment opportunities to the workforce.

Members are active in all types of staffing services, which include professional employer services (employee leasing) managed services (outsourcing), payrolling placement services, temporary-to-full-time services, long-term staffing, and more. NATSS represents more than 1,600 staffing companies that operate approximately 13,000 offices throughout the United States.

Net Temps
http://www.net-temps.com

A popular electronic recruiting site. All advertisements are placed weekly in targeted newsgroups and on Yahoo's series of regional Web sites.

People Lease
http://www.peoplelease.com

People Lease is one of the pioneer of the employee leasing industry. Their services include employee leasing, payroll services, and insurance services. The People Lease system provides scores of companies with a dynamic service that frees them from the burdens of employee administration, and allows them to concentrate on running the business they are really in.

TRAINING

Advanced Personnel Systems
http://www.hrcensus.com

This site has a complete listing of sources of computer based training courseware. Information on HR vendors, products and consultants is also provided.

American Society for Training and Development
http://www.astd.org

Professional association providing leadership for the workplace learning and peformance field.

Association for Human Resource Management
http://www.ahrm.org

Association concerned with training, as well as compensaton, benefits, and relocation.

Association for International Practical Training
http://www.aipt.org

A non-profit organization that promotes international understanding between the U.S. and other countries through on-the-job practical training exchanges for human resource professionals.

Avantos
http://www.avantos.com/team

Report offers advice on conducting multi-source evaulations and automating evaluation systems.

Behavioral Technology
http://www.btweb.com

Strategic selection, performance management, and career development, competency analysis, and competency integration are topics addressed on this site.

Castleman Motivational Institute, Inc.
http://www.cmihub.com

CMI can save meeting and corporate planners time when searching for presenters for seminars, workshops and training sessions. The CMI Hot Hub on the World Wide Web connects decision-makers with professional speakers, seminar leaders, consultants, authors, and related companies.

Planners can search for presenters based on topic, location, industry, or last name. As they browse the Showcase Pages of appropriate presenters, they can also access on-line audio and video clips. The Web site features modest graphics that download quickly, navigational aids to make finding information easy, and Showcase Pages on speakers that include photographs, contact information, services, and references.

Center for the Study of Human Resources
http://www.utexas.edu/research/cshr

The Center's research efforts encompass a wide array of human resource development issues, including training and employment strategies, education (with special emphasis on the role of education in preparing people for work), health, welfare, standards, and incentives.

Clemmer Group
http://www.clemmer-group.com

Provides tools for training, education, and executive development.

Computerworld
http://www.careeragent.com

Web-based tool provides a structured environment for skills and training assessment and professional development.

CPR Education Centre

http://www.ozemail.com.au/~cpredu

This site offers courses, videos, and software for teaching cardiopulmonary resusitation.

CPR+ (CPR Plus)

http://www.cprplusnet.com

CPR+ offers a comprehensive CPR product and service line can be described by three main areas of focus: "Save-A-Life"; "Protect-A-Life"; and "Extend-A-Life". They offer CPR training, first aid, and other health products and services.

Creative Training Techniques

http://www.cttbobpike.com

Employee retention and on-the-job training transfer are the benefits of the participant-centered teaching style used in this company's seminars and products.

CRM Films

http://www.crmfilms.com

Training videos on topics ranging from customer service skills to leadership.

Exellence in Training Corp.

http://www.extrain.com

Source of training materials and supplies.

HR Press Software

http://www.hrpresssoftware.com

Describes software available for employee training and development.

HRD Press

http://www.hrdpress.com

HR development tools (print, video and electronic media) for corporate trainers, consultants, and educators.

Hub Online for Speaking and Training
http://www.cmihub.com

A directory featuring professional trainers and presenters for training programs.

Human Resource Store
http://www.hrstore.com

Provides training tools and outsourcing options for training, recruiting and outplacement services.

Ideations
http://ideations.com

This site offers software, videos, books, reports and a newsletter with tips, activities, learning strategies, lesson plans, games and more to increase training effectiveness.

Interactive Employment Training
http://www.hrtrain.com

Company offers interactive sexual harrassment training on CD-ROM.

J.L. Kellogg Graduate School of Management
http://www.kellogg.nwu.edu

Seminars offered by Northwestern University include strategy and organizational effectiveness and general management.

National Association of Workforce Professionals
http://www.work-web.com/nawdp

Professional association for training, employment, and related fields. Site provides resources and information.

Penn State Executive Programs
http://www.smeal.psu.edu/psep

Courses on diverse management issues.

Presenting Solutions, Inc.

http://www.presol.com

PSI is a computer-based testing and training service offering challenging skills evaluation systems for pre/post training and pre-employment assessment. It provides the temporary staffing industry and corporate human resource departments with software skills evaluation systems for popular PC/Windows and Macintosh platform software applications.

PSG International

http://www.psgintl.com

Human resource and training product provider presents online demonstrations.

Psychology Associates

http://www.Q4solutions.com

A human resource development firm specializing in consulting and training.

Situation Management Systems Inc.

http://www.smsinc.com

Workshops, consulting services, and trainer certification for influence skills development and application.

Training and Development Resource Center

http://www.tcm.com/trdev

Links to many training and development sites, including a variety of vendors, are presented. Information on corporate training and development options using the Internet and e-mail conferencing.

Training and Seminar Locator

http://www.tasl.com

Looking for just the right seminar, short course, certificate program, executive education program, conference, satellite presentation, distance learning program, or training prod-

A Directory of Human Resources Web Sites 209

> **T A S L**
>
> *Training And Seminar Locators*
>
> World Wide Web Address: http://www.tasl.com
>
> **Education, Training and Development Resource Center for Business and Industry**

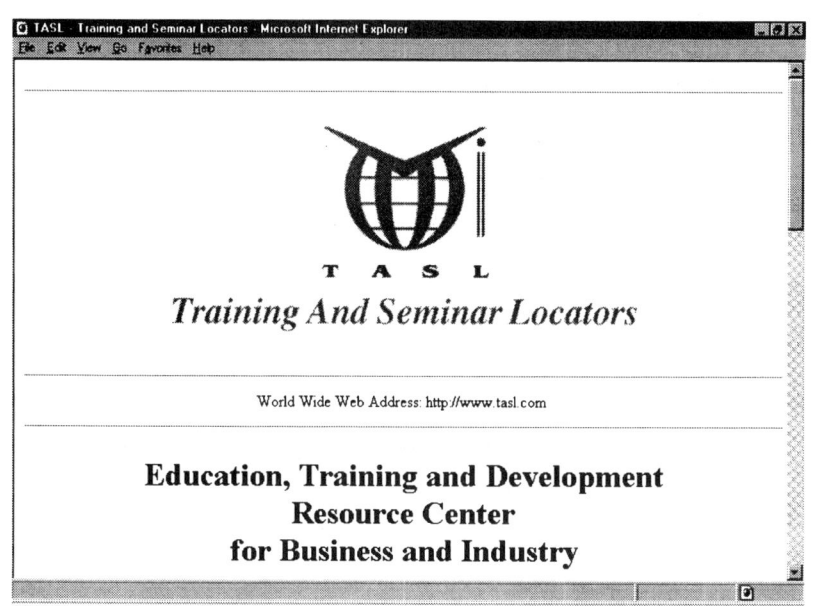

uct? This site has them by the hundreds, from multiple providers, all searchable by keyword. Once you find something promising, you can send the provider an e-mail requesting more information or a proposal.

Training Consortium

http://www.trainingconsortium.com

Options for handling a variety of management training and develoment needs are presented.

Training Forum

http://www.trainingforum.com

Training Forum is a Web site that features comprehensive training and professional information from associations, conference organizers, professional speakers, and consultants. The site includes access to searchable databases, peers and experts for information about tools and techniques for creating and maintaining training materials.

Training Forum's features include a training quote of the day, news, a speakers database, and an events database. A bulletin board service and a database of information on training products is also available.

Training Net

http://www.trainingnet.com/index.cfm

Internet resources for training, human resources, management, and development problems, with a list of training and HR organizations. The event and course finder has details on over 8,000 training and HR events. If you are organizing an HR event, publicize it here at no cost.

Training Source

http://www.rctm.com

The Training Source is a full service resource for video and computer based training materials. They have titles that cover sexual harassment, e-mail, telephone etiquette, and marketing, and much more.

Training Supersite

http://www.trainingsupersite.com

This site brings together in one convenient location all the resources and information which trainers want to find on the Internet. A best bet for all your training and development needs, including books, videos, articles, and much more.

Training Technology Resource Center

http://www.ttrc.doleta.gov

Information on efforts to create high quality, easily-accessible training services.

TRDEVL (Training and Development List)

http://www.intrack.com/intranet

Discussion group facilitates communication between training and development scholars and practitioners.

Usertech

http://www.usertech.com

Provides training, documentation, and performance support programs for integrating people, work, and technology.

Videolearning Systems
http://www.videolrn.com

Video, audio, computer-based training, and CD-ROM programs for staff development are described.

WINGSNET
http://www.vphi.com

Producer and distributor of training videos presents its offerings.

Worklife Strategies
http://www.wd.org/wls/hrfunc.htm

Information on directing the effective management and development of employees.

WEB INDEXES

Alta Vista
http://altavista.digital.com/

Alta Vista is a search engine. This Web address will take you directly to search results for human resources.

Benefits Resources on the Web
http://www.benefitslink.com/?otherbenefits.html

This site has a comprehensive listing of Web sites on a range of benefits topics, from A to Z.

DejaNews
http://www.dejanews.com

Find newsgroups on any topic of interest and view articles from newsgroups.

Employee Relations Web Picks
http://www.nyper.com

Topics covered include labor relations, affirmative action, the Americans with Disabilities Act, collective bargaining, and employment law.

Federal Web Locator

http://www.law.vill.edu/fed-agency

Easy access to a wide range of government information is provided by the links at this site.

Gil Gordon Associates

http://www.gilgordon.com/

If you are considering telecommuting, telework, and alternative officing, this is a valuable site to visit. It presents annotated links to federal, state, local, regional, and rural agencies and projects, associations, vendors, articles, and many other resources.

HR Central

http://www.adia.com/adia/hrcentral.html

This site features a list of Internet sites that deal with human resources and job seeking. The selection reflects sites that are interesting, have good information, and which have links to other good sites.

Included are sites on employee benefits (look here to find out what's new in benefits), HR publications and associations (sites hosted by human resources-related publications and associations), testing and hiring (everything from articles to products for staffing professionals), and job seekers (job posts and advice on resumé writing and interviewing).

HR Online

http://www.hr2000.com

Links to providers of human resource products and services.

HR World

http://www.hrworld.com/

Links to human resource information and resources.

Human Resource Professional's Gateway to the Internet
http://www.teleport.com/~erwilson

Provides links to human resources associations, unions, benefits, training, development, job analysis, personality assessment, employee relations, legal and tax issues, reengineering, occupational health and safety, telecommuting, and workplace learning.

Human Resources Institute
http://hri.eckerd.edu/about.html

The Internet Information Sources page presents hundreds of annotated human resource links in numerous categories.

Human Resources Plaza
http://hodes.com/hr_plaza/hr_11.html

This site provides links to Web sites that publish salary information for various professions in human resources.

Internet HR
http://www.moms.com/hr

Links to a variety of human resource sites.

People Pros, Inc.
http://www.hrimmall.com

Links to sources of information on human resource associations, products, services, and events.

Training and Development Resource Center
http://www.tcm.com/trdev

Links to many training and development sites, including a vareity of vendors, are presented.

Union Resource Network
http://www.unions.org/URN

Index of union websites.

Workforce Online

http://www.workforceonline.com

This site provides many useful human resources links.

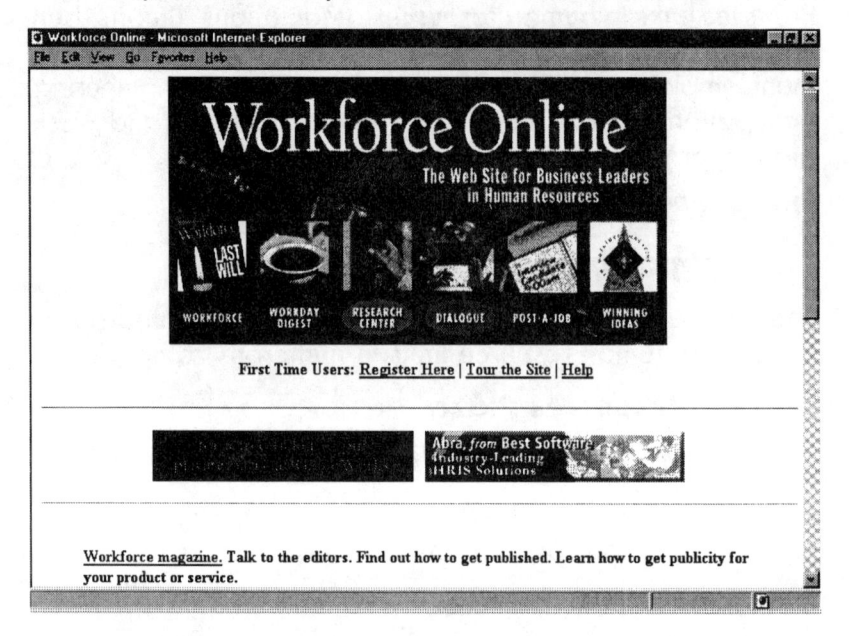

Workindex

http://workindex.com

This comprehensive index of human resources Web sites is a joint venture between Cornell University's School of Industial Labor Relations and *Human Resource Executive* magazine. The index covers a wide range of issues, including HR management, benefits, training, technology, leadership, labor law, compensation, motivation, and relocation. Features include the 10 most noteworthy sites of the month and a menu of new listings, which are added on a monthly basis.

Yahoo

http://www.yahoo.com/business/ corporations/corporate_services/ human_resources/index.html

Yahoo is a search engine which will find whatever subject you are interested in. The human resource category has eighteen general categories: background verification, career and job search services, consulting, drug testing, employee benefits, employee development, employment, employment law, handwriting analysis, insurance, HR associations, outplacement services, professional employer organizations, relocation, sexual harassment, software, training, and workplace safety.

WOMEN'S ISSUES

Bizwomen

http://www.bizwomen.com

Bizwomen is an online interactive community for successful women to communicate, network, exchange ideas and provide support for each other via the Internet. It also includes summaries of news stories dealing with the subject of women and employment.

Equal Opportunity Publications

http://www.eop.com/ccwd/

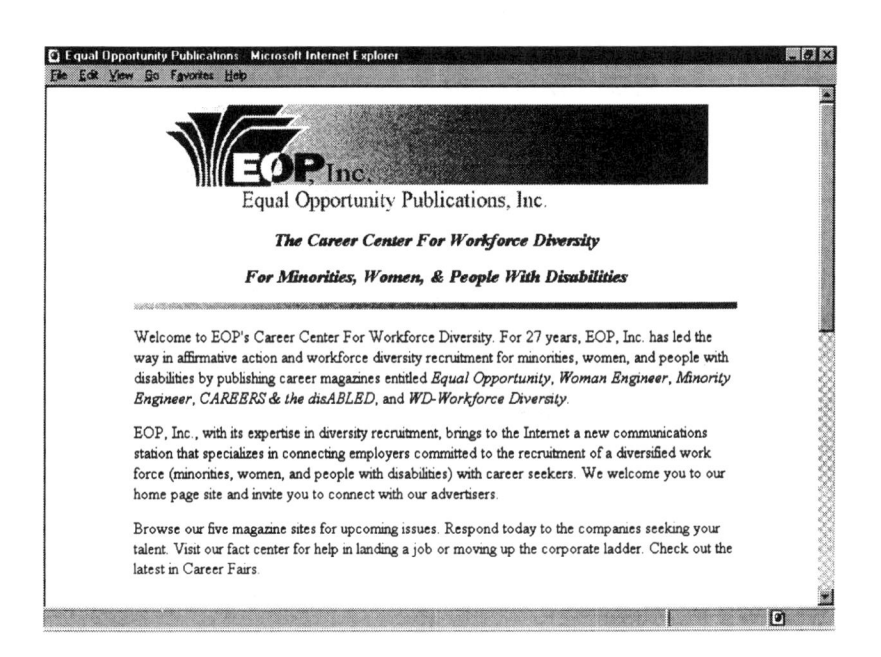

Equal Opportunity Publications, Inc.

The Career Center For Workforce Diversity

For Minorities, Women, & People With Disabilities

Welcome to EOP's Career Center For Workforce Diversity. For 27 years, EOP, Inc. has led the way in affirmative action and workforce diversity recruitment for minorities, women, and people with disabilities by publishing career magazines entitled *Equal Opportunity, Woman Engineer, Minority Engineer, CAREERS & the disABLED,* and *WD-Workforce Diversity.*

EOP, Inc., with its expertise in diversity recruitment, brings to the Internet a new communications station that specializes in connecting employers committed to the recruitment of a diversified work force (minorities, women, and people with disabilities) with career seekers. We welcome you to our home page site and invite you to connect with our advertisers.

Browse our five magazine sites for upcoming issues. Respond today to the companies seeking your talent. Visit our fact center for help in landing a job or moving up the corporate ladder. Check out the latest in Career Fairs.

EOP has a career center for workforce diversity. They publish magazines entitled *Equal Opportunity, Women Engineer, Minority Engineer, Careers and the Disabled* and *Workforce Diversity*.

Sex Discrimination

> http://www.firstfloor.com/catalogs/hr2.htm

A series of articles on sexual discrimination in the workplace, covering comparable worth, dress codes, grooming standards, and pregnancy issues.

US Department of Labor Women's Bureau

> http://www.dol.gov/dol/wb

Information presented on this site includes fact sheets about women in the workplace and statistics on earning differences between men and women.

Women Against Sexual Harassment

> http://www.pic.net/w-a-s-h

WASH is a non-profit corporation formed to assist victims of sexual harassment who do not know where to go for help. This is a site with practical advice from people who have experienced sexual harassment in the workplace.

Women's Web

> http://www.womweb.com

Women's Web is an online resource for individuals who want to learn more about women's issues. It includes information from three well known magazines: *Working Women, Working Mother* and *Ms*.

WORKPLACE VIOLENCE

Amdahl

> http://www.amdahl.com/ext/iacp/pslc1.section2.html

Site provides information on establishing guidelines for a workplace violence program.

American Federation of State, County and Municipal Employees

http://www.afscme.org

Includes information on workplace violence.

Centers for Disease Control

http://www.cdc.gov

A NIOSH fact sheet entitled "Homicide in the Workplace" offers information on which types of workplaces are at highest risk for workplace violence, which weapons are most commonly used, and guidelines on managing an incident.

Family Violence Prevention Fund

http://www.fvpf.org/fund/workplace/home.html

Family violence often spills over into the workplace. The FVPF is a non-profit organization focusing on domestic violence, education, prevention, and public policy reform.

National Crisis Prevention Institute

http://www.execpc.com/~cpi

Provides training in management of disruptive and assaultive behavior, including workshops, seminars, and customized on-site training.

National Trauma Services

http://www.lanz.com/nts/home.htm

Consultants on preventing and responding to workplace violence and trauma. Services include workshops and critical incident stress debriefing.

Stay Out

http://www.stayout.com/violence.html

This article about violence in the workplace explains how widespread this problem is.

Violence at Work

http://www.galaxy.tradewave.com/editors/weiss/WorkSD.html

An extensive collection of links to Web pages with reports, statistics, and resources on workplace violence and how employers and employees can protect themselves.

Voices vs. Violence

http://www.nmha.org/prevention/vvv/index.html

National anti-violence campaign sponsored by the National Mental Health Association.

Workplace Violence Prevention Programs

http://www.dorris.com/wpv.html

Provides assistance in developing policies and procedures.

Workplace Violence Quiz

http://www.mcp.com/60769111715267/phdirect/business/quiz/quiz.html

A series of true/false questions test your knowledge of workplace violence.

CHAPTER 10
WHAT ABOUT...?

CHAPTER 10
WHAT ABOUT...?

As you spend time on the Internet, more questions will arise about how you can get the most out of being online. Here are some of the most common issues that may arise.

AN ADDRESS LISTED IN THIS BOOK DOESN'T WORK. WHY NOT?

The Internet is always changing. People create new resources daily. Resources also disappear or move for countless reasons. Perhaps the person maintaining a Web page lost interest, or moved across the country and changed Internet providers. Or perhaps a company that provided an Internet resource went out of business. It's always disappointing to discover that a great resource has disappeared, but it's a fact of life on the Internet.

Below are a few common problems, and what (if anything) you can do about them.

E-mail

If you send an electronic mail message and it doesn't successfully reach its destination, you will receive a message from **MAILER-DAEMON**, a computer program that reports delivery problems. If the message from **MAILER-DAEMON** says "user unknown," then the account that you are trying to reach (the part before the @ symbol of the recipient's e-mail address) is not valid. If the **MAILER-DAEMON** states "host unknown," then the site you are trying to reach (the part after the @ symbol) is not valid.

If the user is unknown, you might try sending e-mail to **postmaster@** that host, and asking nicely where the recipient went. There isn't much you can do if the host is invalid, since the computer is simply gone. But do make sure that you typed the e-mail address correctly when you sent the message. Computers are finicky about spelling, including punctuation in an address.

World Wide Web and Gopher

It seems that Web sites come, go, and move faster than other types of Internet resources. Perhaps is just appears that way because there are more Web sites than any other type of Internet resource.

If your Web browser says it is "unable to locate the server" or that the server "has no DNS entry," then the Web site you are trying to access is gone. If your browser complains that the site "is unavailable" or "is not accepting connections," this isn't as bad. These messages mean that the site you are trying to access exists, but the Web server is currently offline or otherwise preoccupied. Try again in a little while, and it may connect.

If your browser complains that the page you are after is "not found," it means that the site does exist, but the specific Web page you're seeking isn't there. It may not be gone for good, however. The Web site may simply have been reorganized, and the information you want has been moved. You might try e-mailing **webmaster@** that site and politely asking where it went. Or you might try backing up a directory or two to the site's top-level page and see if you can locate it from there by following links.

If all else fails, remember that the Web page you are looking for may have moved or may be duplicated elsewhere on the Internet. Use an Internet search tool like InfoSeek, Excite, WebCrawler, or Lycos to search for the page's new location.

Newsgroups

USENET newsgroups are rather stable. Once created, it is rare that a newsgroup will ever disappear. Newsgroups do sometimes get reorganized, and their names can get changed in the process. This should pose no problem to newgroupies, though, because the new offspring are usually easy to track down.

WHAT IS LEGAL TO PUT ON THE INTERNET?

Because the explosive growth of the Internet is such a recent phenomenon, the legal issues surrounding this communications medium are nebulous and highly controversial. The main issues of concern are copyright laws and the matter of posting or transmitting socially questionable material.

The current copyright law is the Copyright Act of 1976, which protects "items of expression," including literary, dramatic, artistic, and musical works. Basically, all original expression is copyright-protected as soon as it assumes a tangible form. What constitutes a "tangible" form on the Net is debateable. It can be argued that the very nature of how the Internet works causes copyright infringements all the time.

The legal issues are still being studied and debated, but here are a few guidelines to follow based on the current laws and common sense:

- Assume that all original text content of Web pages, e-mail, and USENET messages, as well as sound and graphics files, executable computer programs, and computer program listings, are protected by copyright law. Don't copy and re-post any original content unless you have explicit permission from the author.
- Some types of material are not eligible for copyright protection, such as ideas, facts, titles, names, short phrases, and blank forms. You may use these materials in your Internet content and transmissions.

- The Fair Use Provision of the Copyright Act permits exemptions from copyright law, as long as the copied material is used or redistributed for academic, journalistic, or satirical purposes.
- You may include lists of hyperlinks in your Internet material. A link to a URL is analogous to a written street address, which is not copyrightable. However, someone else's value-added list of links is protected from copyright infringement. Therefore, you may incorporate hyperlinks into your Internet content, but you may not copy someone else's entire compilation.
- If you would like to use someone else's copyrighted material but aren't sure you can do so legally, it doesn't hurt to contact the copyright owner and ask for permission.

For more information, refer to The Copyright Website (***http://www.benedict.com/***).

ARE THERE RULES ON HOW TO COMMUNICATE ON THE INTERNET?

Communicating on the Internet is several steps removed from person-to-person communication. It is imperative to follow guidelines in order to maintain good relationships with your Internet correspondents and service provider. While netiquette is not legally binding, it is important to learn and abide by these rules in order to avoid misunderstandings, ostracism, and revoked Internet privileges.

Most rules of netiquette are based on good manners, technical understanding, and common sense. Netiquette for the various Internet protocols, such as e-mail, USENET newsgroups, IRC, TELNET, and the World Wide Web, conforms to some general guidelines as well as to specific codes for each particular medium. The codes of netiquette usually fall into three interrelated categories: social conduct, technical courtesy, and harmful behavior.

Social conduct. When composing messages to be transmitted via e-mail, USENET newsgroups, or interactive chat media, you should behave in a respectful manner, just as you would while communicating in person. The inability to physically see or hear each other does not free you of personal responsibility. For example, avoid typing your messages in all capital letters because it appears as if you are SHOUTING. This is a major pet peeve for most veteran Internet users.

Technical courtesy. Be aware and respectful of your fellow user and Internet service providers' technical limitations. Do not use more than your fair share of system resources by exceeding your allotted disk storage allowance or consuming massive amounts of bandwidth in order to send digitized home movies to your friends with slow modems. Keep your posted messages concise and avoid disseminating volumes of your opinions to uninterested or inappropriate audiences.

Harmful behavior. The worst breach of netiquette is to hurt someone with obscene or culturally offensive behavior or to cause damage to someone else's computer or network system. Breaches can occur accidentally, such as in the case of unwittingly distributing a virus-infected program. However, the established Internet community believes that perpetrators should assume responsibility for learning how to avoid these types of problems.

The codes of netiquette are simple to follow, so take the time to learn them. If you do, you will find your Internet experiences to be both pleasant and rewarding. Refer to ***http://www.fau.edu/rinaldi/netiquette.html*** for a complete guide to netiquette.

SHOULD I WORRY ABOUT THE PRIVACY OF MY INTERNET TRANSMISSIONS?

The Internet is a preferred mode of communication for a growing number of people. Internet communication is expanding into every aspect of life, so many people are concerned with protecting the privacy of their Internet content and transmissions. The Internet, by its very nature, however, is not a secure network. In fact, it is designed to be as open and publicly accessible as possible. There are ways to ensure the security of your information, but no method is failsafe.

Most Internet servers employ some degree of security to protect material from nosy and malicious hackers. But again, there is no fool-proof sure way to protect information.

How Can I Ensure the Privacy of What I Send Via the Internet?

If you want your Internet communications to be public information, such as you message posting in a USENET newsgroup or your Web home page, the content must merely be protected from destruction by mischievous hackers and viruses. Check with your Internet Service Provider to find out its methods for protecting its information servers. If you are sending personal information you wish to protect, such as your credit card number, home address, or telephone number, there are some precautions you may take to secure that information.

Currently, there are two basic methods of transmitting private information. One is to send content over the Net by way of a secured protocol. Some examples include the Secure Hypertext Transport Protocol (S-HTTP), Netscape Netsite's Secured Sockets Layer (SSL), and Secure Newsgroups. The other method involves the sender encrypting the information and then sending the encrypted data, and the receiving party decrypting the material.

One tool you can use to encrypt data is Pretty Good Privacy (PGP), which is freely available and widely supported. Refer to **http://draco.centerline.com:8080/~franl/ pgp/documentation.html** for more information about PGP. The best way to ensure security, however, is to employ a combination of these methods, thereby encrypting both the content and the transmission itself.

Even if you are a law-abiding citizen with nothing to hide, you may choose to keep your Internet content and transmissions private. For more information about Internet security, cryptography, and privacy, refer to the Netsurfer Focus on Cryptography and Privacy Web site at **http://www.netsurf.com/nsf/v01/03/nsf.01.03.html.**

Is It Safe to Send My Credit Card Number Over the Internet?

Some people feel say that using a credit card is fine. Others think that the Net is full of people trying to steal credit card numbers and never send their card numbers across the Net.

But do you ever order from a catalog and give your credit card number over a cordless or cellular phone? Have you ever thrown away a receipt from a credit card purchase without shredding it? Have you every left a restaurant or store with only your receipt, leaving the carbon behind? Yes, in theory it is possible for some ambitious and highly talented person to grab your unencrypted account number off the Net. And some encryption today is embarrassingly easy to break. But don't consider credit card transactions on the Net to be any more dangerous than most other credit card transactions.

WHAT DO I NEED TO KNOW ABOUT COMPUTER VIRUSES?

A computer virus is a program that maliciously causes unwanted behavior on a computer. Viruses replicate themselves on computer systems by incorporating themselves into other programs shared among computer systems. Viruses are created by rogue programmers who distribute them and watch them spread.

The term "computer virus" was coined because these programs have similar attributes to a biological virus. Computer viruses have three defining qualities in common:
- The ability to replicate themselves.
- The requirement of a "carrier" or "host".

- The capacity to damage or cause unexpected behavior on infected computer systems.

The intentions of a computer virus program range from being harmless and humorous to causing damage. Some viruses cause the computer screen to display silly animation or messages, while others delete the contents of an entire hard disk.

Computer viruses do exist and are passed around, both intentionally and unintentionally. Your computer can catch a virus from an infected program downloaded from the Internet via FTP, Web sites, or e-mail attachments, from a bulletin board system, or on a disk handed to you by a friend, or by accessing an infected hard drive. To learn more about the various types of viruses, visit **http://www.einet.net/ galaxy/Engineering-and-Technology/Computer-Technology/Security/davidhull/intro.htm** and read "Safe Hex for the Nineties."

Each virus is unique, so you should use reliable, up-to-date virus scanner software. A virus scanner is a program that is designed to check an entire computer system for known viruses or suspicious activity. There are many free virus scanners available, such as Disinfectant for the Macintosh (**http://hyperarchive.lcs.mit.edu/HyperArchive/Abstracts/vir/HyperArchive.html**), or McAfee VirusScan for DOS/Windows (**http://www.mcafee.com/**).

Finally, be sure to learn about hardware write-protect methods and to implement a reliable backup system to use in case of an emergency. For more information about computer viruses, refer to the VIRUS-Lcomp.virus FAQ at **http://www.umcc.umich.edu/~doug/virus-faq.html** or http://www.cis.ohio-state.edu/hypertext/faq/usenet/computer-virus-faq/faq.html.

HOW CAN A HUMAN RESOURCES PROFESSIONAL CREATE A WEB PAGE?

So you're ready to create your own World Wide Web page. You've got something to say, and if that something needs to

What About ...?

be said on the Web, then the only things standing between you and your very own Web page are a Web server and HTML (HyperText Markup Language).

As you work on your Web site, you don't even need to connect to a World Wide Web server to look at your creation yourself. Most Web browsers let you read an HTML file right from your hard disk if the page isn't yet on the Web.

IS THERE A LOT OF PORNOGRAPHY ON THE INTERNET?

There is some porn on the Internet, but you are unlikely to find it by accident. There are Web sites, newsgroups, and FTP sites filled with pornographic or sexually explicit material. Most of these sites contain soft-core pictures and stories, although some of the material is much more explicit.

However, people who believe that the Internet is nothing more than a haven for pedophiles and weirdos to swap pictures are misguided and misinformed. It is important to keep in mind that the Internet is a reflection of our society as a whole. There are pornographic pictures on the Internet because that's what some people are interested in. This material is only a small portion of the information found on the Net. Information of more redeeming value far outweighs the volume of "dirty" pictures.

Chapter 11
WHAT DOES THAT MEAN?

Chapter 11

WHAT DOES THAT MEAN?

The Internet uses many terms and acronyms which are unfamiliar to non-Net users. Here are some terms you'll encounter as you continue your explorations of the Net.

Bandwidth: The maximum amount of data, measured in bits per second (bps), that can be sent through a network.

Base 64: A standard for packaging data for transfer.

Baud rate: Measure of rate of speed of flow of information between devices, measured in bits per second.

Bits per second (bps): A measure of the speed at which data is transmitted. Often used to rate the speed of modems.

Bps: *See* Bits per second.

Client: A computer which requests a file server to provide data.

Cookies: Files left by web sites on client computers intended to register user preferences if the site is accessed again.

CSLIP: Compressed Serial Line Interface Protocol. *See* Serial Line Interface Protocol.

Domain type: The suffix at the end of an Internet address which includes indicates the type of organization the address represents. Examples are .com (for commercial users),

.edu (for colleges, universities, and other educational institutions), .gov (for government agencies), .net (for network providers), .mil (for military users) and .org (for other organizations). For example, .com is the domain type in the address hrmanager@AOL.com. Outside the U.S., domain types are used to note the country the user is located in (example: .ca is used for Canada).

Download: Copying data or software from a host computer to your computer.

Electronic mail (E-mail) address: The Internet address, such as 74644.3017@compuserve.com, to which e-mail messages are sent.

Electronic mail (E-mail) system: The system by which computer users can exchange text messages and files with other users.

E-mail: See Electronic Mail.

Emoticons: A collection of symbols used to express emotions in e-mail messages. Common examples are :-) (smile), :-((frown), :-o (surprise) and :-D (laugh). (Turn page lengthwise to better view these symbols.)

Encryption: A method of data protection that allows only the intended recipient to see the data.

FAQ: See Frequently Asked Questions.

File server: A computer handling data management for a client computer.

File Transfer Protocol (FTP): The networking standard that allows a user to transfer files to and from the Internet.

Flame: A critical comment directed at another person in a newsgroup or a chat session.

Frame: A separate window within the main window of a Web browser that contains a different HTML document.

Freeware: Software you can download and use for free.

Frequently Asked Questions (FAQ): A file provided by many newsgroups so that new users can have their questions answered without general postings.

FTP: *See* File Transfer Protocol.

GIF: *See* Graphic Interchange Format.

Graphic Interchange Format (GIF): A multi-platform, bit-mapped graphics format that was the first graphics standard on the World Wide Web.

Gopher: A menu-based tool for locating information on the Internet.

Home page: The introductory page of a Web site.

Host: A computer to which other computers on a network are connected.

HTML: *See* Hypertext Markup Language.

HTTP: *See* Hypertext Transport Protocol.

Hypertext: A text string on a Web page that provides links to other pages on the Internet. Hypertext usually is displayed in a different color and is underlined.

Hypertext Markup Language (HTML): The coding language for creating hypertext documents on the Web.

Hypertext Transport Protocol (HTTP): The standard establishing communications procedures between Web clients and servers.

Integrated Services Digital Network (ISDN): A digital telephone standard providing faster, noise-free data transfer compared to normal phone lines.

Internet: The world's largest network, consisting of computers and the connections between them.

Internet Relay Chat (IRC): The protocol that allows real-time chat across the Internet.

Internet Service Provider (ISP): A company that sells access to the Internet.

Intranet: The application of Web technology to internal company or organization computer networks.

IRC: *See* Internet Relay Chat.

ISDN: *See* Integrated Services Digital Network.

ISP: *See* Internet Service Provider.

Java: An object-oriented, multi-platform programming language whose features make it the preferred language for developing applications on the World Wide Web.

JPEG: A graphics file format developed by the Joint Photographics Experts Group (JPEG) which uses a compression algorithmn to reduce the size of digital photos and pictures.

Kbps: Thousand bits per second. *See* bps.

Lurking: Reading postings from others in newsgroups or chat rooms without actively participating.

Mailing lists: A list of individuals sending and receiving information via e-mail on a specific topic on a regular basis.

Mirror site: A site that contains the same contents as another site; used to decrease user traffic on the other site.

MIME: *See* Multipurpose Internet Mail Extensions.

Modem: A device that allows your computer to transmit and receive data over the Internet.

Multipurpose Internet Mail Extensions (MIME): A file transfer protocol which establishes how different types of e-mail are packaged and electronically labeled.

Netiquette: The rules of behavior for communicating online.

Network News Transfer Protocol (NNTP): The standard used by newsreader software to access newsgroups.

Newsgroup: A series of Internet postings devoted to the discussion of a particular topic.

Newsgroup post: A typed opinion or comment sent to a newsgroup. Also called a posting.

Newsgroup reader: Software designed to display and navigate newsgroup postings.

NNTP: *See* Network News Transfer Protocol.

Offline: Any work performed on a computer that is not connected to the Internet or an online service.

Online: Any work performed on a computer that is connected to the Internet or an online service.

Online service: A commercial service that provides e-mail, news, information, entertainment, or Internet access to subscribers.

Packet: A unit of data sent across the Internet.

Point-to-Point Protocol (PPP): An Internet standard governing the transfer of data over modems and phone lines.

POTS: Plain Old Telephone Service. Compare with ISDN.

PPP: *See* Point-to-Point Protocol.

Protocol: A software specification to establish the rules and procedures for communication between computers.

Quoting: Copying part of an original e-mail or newsgroup message in your reply message; a greater-than symbol (>) usually precedes any lines of a quote.

Router: A computer or software package that forwards a packet toward its destination. A packet may travel through several routers before finishing its journey.

Search engine: A software program that uses a keyword or directory structure to search the Web for relevant sites.

Serial Line Interface Protocol (SLIP): Internet protocol which establishes how data is sent via modems and phone lines.

Server: *See* File server.

Shareware: Software you can download and use on a trial basis before deciding whether to purchase it.

Shouting: Writing e-mail messages using only captial letters instead of upper and lower case letters is considering shouting. It should be avoided. Emoticons should be used instead.

SLIP: *See* Serial Line Interface Protocol.

Snail mail: Slang for postal service.

TCP/IP: *See* Transmission Control Protocol/Internet Protocol.

Transmission Control Protocol/Internet Protocol (TCP/IP): The network standard that dictates how information is sent across the Internet.

Universal Resource Locator (URL): The address of a Web site.

Unix-to-Unix Encode (uuencode): A standard for packaging data for transfer.

Upload: Copying data or software from your computer to a host computer. Uploading copyrighted, commercial software is illegal.

URL: *See* Universal Resource Locator.

USENET: *See* User's Network.

User name: The name you use when connecting to the Internet. Also called a user ID.

User's Network (USENET): A worldwide network of newsgroups.

Uuencode: *See* Unix-to-Unix Encode.

Veronica: *See* Very Easy Rodent-Oriented Net-wide Index to Computerized Archives

Very Easy Rodent-Oriented Net-wide Index to Computerized Archives (Veronica): A popular tool for searching Gopherspace.

WAIS: *See* Wide Area Information Service.

Web browser: The software that communicates with and displays the information on a Web page.

Web page: A document that can be accessed on the Internet. A Web page may contain text, hypertext links, graphics, video, and audio.

Web site: A series of interconnected Web pages, usually created and operated by one person or organization.

Wide Area Information Server (WAIS): A Gopherspace search engine.

World Wide Web (WWW): Often shortened to Web, it is the body of text, graphics, video, and audio data accessible on the Internet. The Web is characterized by its use of hyperlinks.

WWW: *See* World Wide Web.

INDEX

Abbott, Langer & Associates Management Consultants, 132
Academy of Human Resource Development, 135
Academy of Management, 116
Access Business Online, 131-132
Access Corporation, 188
Accountemps, 202
ADA, *see* Americans with Disabilities Act
ADA-Law, 79
Addiction, 79, 113-114
Addict-L, 79
Addresses, *see* Electronic mail
Administaff, 202
Administrative address, 24, 70-72
Advanced Benefit Services, 123
Advanced query functions, 104
Advanced Personnel Systems, 189, 204
Advanced Research Projects Agency Network (ARPANET), 5, 12
Aetna, 123
Affam-L, 80
Affirmative action, 80, 114-115
AFL-CIO LaborWeb, 157
AFSCME, 180, 217
Again Technologies, 132, 189
Agency for Toxic Substances and Disease Registry, 180

Alexander Information Group, 185
All Business Network, 140-142, 159-160, 173, 185
ALMIS Home Page, 199
Alt, 67-68
Alt.business.insurance, 77
Alt.education-disabled, 77
Alt.manufacturing.misc, 77
Alt.sexual.abuse.recovery, 78
Alt.society.labor-unions, 78
Alt.support, 78
Alt.support.non-smokers, 78
Alta Vista, 103-104, 211
Alternative dispute resolution, 80, 165-167
Alternative staffing, 202-204
Amdahl, 216-217
America Online (AOL), 16, 25, 33-34
American Arbitration Association of Dispute Resolution Services, 116, 165-166
American Association for Affirmative Action, 114, 117, 160
American Association of Colleges and Employers, 117, 173
American Compensation Association, 116, 133
American Council on International Personnel, 117-118
American Dental Association, 123-124
American Federation of State, County and Municipal Employees, 180, 217
American Marketing Association, 118
American National Standards Institute, 181
American Productivity and Quality Center, 118, 172
American Psychological Association, 160, 187
American Society for Industrial Security, 118, 184-185
American Society for Quality Control, 118, 172
American Society for Training and Development, 118, 135-136, 204
American Society of Pension Actuaries, 118-119, 124
Americans with Disabilities Act, 78, 79, 80, 137-139,

141, 143-144
America's Job Bank, 173
Ameritest, 113
Amsquare, 151
Anonymous FTP, 102
AOL, see America Online
Application Group, 189
Application Profiles, 185
Archie, 99-100
Armor Personnel, 202
ARPANET, see Advanced Research Projects Agency Network
Assessment, 116
Assessment Systems Inc., 116, 185
Association for Human Resource Management, 119, 204
Association for International Practical Training, 204
Association for Worksite Health Promotion, 147
Associations, 116-122
At, 90
AT&T World Net Services, 44
Au, 90
Austin-Hayne Corp., 189
Austria, 90
Australia, 83, 90
Automatic Data Processing, 171, 189

Backbone, 14
Background checks, 185-187, 190
Bandwidth, 233
Base64, 58, 233
Baud rate, 233
Behavior at work, 122-123
Behavioral Technology, 204-205
Benefit Design Inc., 124
Benefit Software Inc, 124, 189-190
Benefit Systems Technologies, 124-125
Benefits, 80, 123-131

Benefits Advantage, 125
Benefits-L, 80
Benefits Resources on the Web, 211
BenefitsLink, 125
Berger Law Office, 137, 160
Berkshire Associates, 114, 143, 190
Bernard Hodes Advertising, 150, 173
Best Software, 190
Bigfoot, 58
Bits per second, 30-31, 233
Biz, 67-68, 146
Biz.general, 78
Biz.jobs.offered, 78
Biz.listserv.ada.law, 78
Biz.listserv.quality, 78
Bizwomen, 215
Blair Mill Administrators Inc., 125
Bookmarks, 48
Bps, *see* bits per second
Bureau of Economic Analysis, 198-199
Bureau of Labor Statistics, 125, 133, 199
BUSHEA, 80
Business Enterprise Trust, 119
Business information, 131-132
Business insurance, 77

.ca, 23, 90
Caras & Associates Inc., 141, 166
CARDEVNET, 80
Career Atlas for the Road, 151
Career Crafting, 151
Career development, 80
Career Dynamics, 152
Career Magazine, 152
Career Management International, 152
Career Mart, 152
Career Mosaic, 173

Career Planning Process, 152
Career Shop, 152-153
Career Web, 153, 174
Careernet, 80
Careerpath, 152, 173-174
Careers, 80
Carpal Tunnel Syndrome Page, 145
Castleman Motivational Institute Inc., 205
Catalog of Federal Domestic Assistance, 125
Center for the Study of Human Resources, 205
Centers for Disease Control, 181, 217
Centra Software, 190
Certified Systems Inc., 202-203
Change, 80
Chat, 25, 72-74
Checksums, 57
Chevron lawsuit, 59
CIC Applicant Background Checks, 185, 190
Citibank lawsuit, 59
Clari.biz.industry.services, 78
Clari.news.smoking, 78
Clari.news.usa.law, 78
Clari.news.women, 78
Clayton Wallis Co., 190
Clemmer Group, 205
Client, 233
Client-server, 89
CNN.FN, 167
Code of Federal Regulations, 162-163
Cohen & Associates Agencies, 126
Collegegrad, 153
Collin W. Fritz and Associates, 126
.com, 23, 55, 89
Communications Briefings, 141
Communicator, *see* Netscape
Comp, 66
Compensation, 133-135

Compensation Planning Software, 133
Complete Intranet Resource, 151
Compressed SLIP (CSLIP), 45-46, 233 (*see also* Serial Line Interface Protocol)
CompuServe, 5, 25, 34-35
Computer viruses, 227-228
Computerworld, 205
Connections
   Dedicated, 40-41
   Dial-up direct connection, 41
   Dial-up Serial Line Internet Protocol (SLIP)/Point-to-Point Protocol (PPP) account, 41
   Dial-up Terminal Emulation, 41
Consultant Team Inc., 190-191
Consulting, 79, 163-165
Cookies, 233
Copyright Act of 1976, 223
   Fair Use provision, 224
Copyright issues, 223-224
Copyright Website, 224
CORE Inc., 126, 137
Cornell Institute of Collective Bargaining, 158
Cornell University, 126, 142, 158, 160, 167
Cornell University Center for Advanced Human Resource Studies, 167
Cornell University Legal Information Institute, 160
Cornell University School of Industrial and Labor Relations, 158
Cornell Work and Environment Institute, 158
Counseling services, 135
Court TV, 137-138, 141, 158-159, 160, 186
CPR Education Centre, 206
CPR Plus, 206
Creative Training Techniques, 206
Credit card numbers, 227
Criterion Inc., 115, 191
CRM Films, 206

CSBAN, 116
CSLIP, see Compressed SLIP
CTD News Online, 145
CTDs, see Cumulative Trauma Disorders
Cumulative Trauma Disorders, 84, 145
Cyber Accountant, 200
Cybernetics, 191
Cyborg Systems, 126, 191

DATAIR Employment Benefit Systems Inc., 126-127
Dedicated connections, 40-41
DejaNews, 69, 153, 211
Demographic Data Viewer, 199
Denison University Campus Security and Safety, 181
Department of Agriculture, 149
Department of Energy, 184
Department of Health and Human Services, 149-150
Department of Justice, 137, 162
Department of Labor, 125-126, 133-134, 144, 156, 183, 216
Department of Labor Women's Bureau, 144, 216
Depaul University, 147
Development, 135-137
Development Dimensions International, 136
Dial-up direct connection, 41
Dial-up Internet protocols, 41, 44-46
Dial-up Serial Line Internet Protocol (SLIP)/Point-to-Point Protocol (PPP) account, 41
Dial-up Terminal Emulation, 41
Digests, 70
Dilbert Zone, 167
Disabilities, 77, 78, 79
Disability, 137-139
Disability Etiquette Handbook, 138, 144
Disinfectant for the Macintosh, 228
Dispute-Res, 80
Dispute resolution, 80, 165-167

Dispute Resolution and Conflict Avoidance for the Construction Industry, 166
Diversity, 80, 81, 139-140
Domain types, 23, 233-234
Download, 234
Dreyfuss Hunt, 147-148
Duke University Human Resources, 146
Duke University Occupational and Environmental Medicine, 181
Dun & Bradstreet, 131

E-Benefits, 127
E-mail, *see* Electronic mail
EAP, 81
Edify—Electronic Workforce, 191
.edu, 23, 55, 89
Education, 77
Electronic mail, 9, 24-25, 53-61, 221-222, 234
    Address format, 55, 234
    Attachments, 57
    Capabilities of, 53-54
    Error messages, 221-222
    Etiquette, 60-61
    Finding addresses, 58-59
    MIME, see Multi-purpose Internet Mail Extensions
    Popularity of, 53-54
    Racism via, 59-60
    Sending, 24-25, 55-56
    Sexual harrassment via, 59
    Software, 56-57
    System, 234
    Shouting, 60
Electronic Recruiting News, 174
Emergency Preparedness Information Exchange, 181
Emoticons, 234
Employee assistance, 81, 119, 127
Employee Asssistance Professionals Association, 119,

Index

127
Employee Benefit Research Institute, 119, 127
Employee ownership, 140
Employee relations, 115, 140-143
Employee Relations Web Picks, 115, 138, 141, 211-212
Employee Relocation Council, 179
Employment discrimination, 143-144
Employment Testing and Screening, 186
Encryption, 226-227, 234
Environmental Protection Agency, 181-182
Environmental Resource Center, 182
Equal Opportunity Publications, 115, 138, 139, 215-216
Equipment requirements, 29-31
Ergonomics, 84, 145
Ergoware Products, 145
ErgoWeb, 145
ERIC Clearinghouse on Adult, Career and Vocational Education, 153
Error messages, 221-222
E-SPAN, 153
Eudora, 54, 56-57
Excellence in Training, 206
Exchange, see Microsoft
Excite, 104-105
Executive development, 83
Explorer, see Microsoft

Fair Use, 232
Family Violence Prevention Fund, 217
FAQ, see Frequently Asked Questions
Federal Emergency Management Agency, 182
Federal Employee's Survival Guide, 155-156
Federal Register, 182
Federal Web Locator, 212
FedWorld, 182-183
FedWorld Federal Jobs Announcement Search, 154
Fidelity Investments, 127

File server, 234
File Transfer Protocol (FTP), 21, 23, 101-102, 234
Find Law—Labor Law, 138, 161
Flame, 234
Flexible work hours, 81
Flexwork, 81
Focus Groups, 142
Foundation for Enterprise Development, 119, 140, 159
Four11.com, 58
Frames, 47, 234
Freeware, 234
Frequently Asked Questions, 11, 221, 235
Friend and Walker, 122
FTP, see File Transfer Protocol

Gay Workplace Issues, 127, 144
Genelco Inc., 191
Genesys Systems Software, 191-192
George Mason University, 146
GIF, see Graphic Interchange Format
Gil Gordon Associates, 201, 212
Global Human Resource Services Ltd., 163-164
G-Niel Companies, 8, 167
Golden Gophers, 96
Gopher, 22, 96-101, 235
Gopherspace, 22, 96
.gov, 23, 55, 90
Government Information Locator Service, 199
Government Institutes, 183
Government Printing Office, 161
Grantsmanship Center, 119-120
Graphic Interchange Format (GIF), 235
Greentree Systems, 174
Griggs Productions Inc., 139, 192

Harassment Hotline, 187-188
Harmful behavior, 224-225

Hazelden, 113, 148
Health, 147-150
Health and Human Services Agencies, 127-128
Health Care Financing Adminstration, 148
Health promotion, 147-150
Heart Advertising Network, 174
Hierarchies, 66-68
H-Labor, 81
Hodes Advertising, 150, 173
Home page, 19, 235
Hoover Business Profiles, 131-132
House of Representatives Internet Law Library, 162-163
Host, 235
HotMail, 59
HR and Compensation Systems Census, 192
HR Central, 212
HR Investment Consultants, 128
HR Manager, 168
HR Online, 168, 212
HR Plus, 186
HR Power Guide, 168
HR Press Software, 136, 192, 206
HR World, 212
HRD Press, 206
HRD-L, 81
HRIS-L, 81
HRM-One, 171
HRNET, 81
HR-OD-L, 81
HTML, *see* Hypertext Markup Language
HTTP, *see* Hypertext Transfer Protocol
Hub Online for Speaking and Training, 207
Human Resource Development Network, 136
Human Resource Development Press, 168
Human Resource Law Website, 161
Human Resource MicroSystems, 192
Human Resource Professional's Gateway to the Internet,

213
Human Resource Store, 171, 207
Human Resources Headquarters, 168
Human Resources Institute, 120, 168-169, 213
Human Resources Management Systems, 169
Human Resources Planning Society, 120
Human Resources Plaza, 134, 169, 213
  Reading Room, 169
Humanic Design, 192
Hunter Group, 164, 192-193
Hyperlinks, 88-89
Hypertext, 235
Hypertext Markup Language, 89, 229, 235
Hypertext Transport Protocol, 23, 89, 235

IBN, 174
ICONtrol Inc., 172
Ideations, 207
IERN-L, 82
IETF, *see* Internet Engineering Task Force
Illinois Employment and Training Center, 154
Impact Consulting Group, 164
Industrial psychology, 82
Industrial relations, 82, 120
Industrial Relations Research Association, 82, 120
Information Learning Systems, 193
Information superhighway, 6
Information Technology Support Center, 128
Informus Employment Screening, 186
Infoseek, 20, 105-106
Institute of Collective Bargaining, 142, 158
Institute of Management and Administration, 120
Insurance, 77
Integrated Services Digital Network (ISDN), 31-32, 235
Integrity Center, 187
Interactive Corp., 129
Interactive Employment Training, 188, 207
Interactive multimedia, 88

Internal Revenue Service, 201
International Association for Human Resource Information Management-USA, 120, 193
International Foundation of Employee Benefits Plans, 120, 129
International Organization for Standardization, 172
International Personnel Management Association, 82, 121, 122
Internet, 3-7, 12-13, 29-31, 44-46, 49, 74, 95-96, 235
   Definition of, 3-4, 12, 235
   Equipment requirements, 29-31
   History of, 4-6, 12
   Privacy, 226-227
   Protocols, 5, 44-46, 95-96, 234, 236, 237
   Reasons for using, 17-20
   Security, 49, 225-227
   Size of, 13
   Users of, 6-7
   Voice communication over, 74
Internet Address Finder, 58
Internet Engineering Task Force (IETF), 22
Internet Explorer, *see* Microsoft
Internet in a Box, 42
Internet MCI, 44
Internet News, see Microsoft
Internet Relay Chat (IRC), 25, 72-73, 235
Internet Resources, Types of, 17
Internet Service Providers (ISPs), 12, 14, 169, 235
   Choosing, 39-44
   Differences between Online Services and, 15-16, 32-33, 41
   Phone companies as, 44
Internet Society (ISOC), 13
Inter-Network Mail Guide, 55-56
Intersourcing Online, 179
Interviewing Skills, 154
InTime Solutions, 193

Intranet Journal, 151
Intranets, 150-151, 188, 191, 192 236
IOOB-L, 82
IPMAAC-List, 82
IRC, see Internet Relay Chat
IRRA, 82
ISDN, see Integrated Services Digital Network
ISOC, see Internet Society
ISPs, see Internet Service Providers

Janweb, 138, 144, 174
Java, 236
J.L. Kellogg Graduate School of Management, 207
Job Accomodation Network, 138, 144, 174
Job analysis, 82
Job search techniques, 82, 151-157
Jobanalysis, 82
Jobplace, 82
Jobs, 78, 79, 84
JobSmart, 134, 175
Job-tech, 82
Joint Photographics Expert Group (JPEG), 236
.jp, 23
JPEG, see Joint Photographics Expert Group
Jungian Personality Test, 187
Juno, 59

Kaplan Career Center, 154
Kbps, 236
Keirsey Temperament Sorter, 187
Kelley Services, 175
Kellogg Graduate School of Management, 207
KPMG, 193

Labnews, 83
Labor history, 81
Labor-L, 83

Index 255

Labor-management relations, 157-159
Labor unions, 78, 83, 84
Law, 78, 79, 159-163
Lawson Software, 193
Lee Hecht Harrison, 170, 175
Library of Congress, 161
List, The, 42
List of Top 1000 US Companies, 132
Listservs, *see* Mailing lists
Liszt Email Discussion Group Directory, 159, 166
LMI Net, 199
Logical Design Solutions, 194
Lurking, 24, 236
Lycos, 106-107

Mailer daemon, 221-222
Mailing lists, 24, 69-72, 79-84, 224-225, 236
   Administrative address, 24, 70-72
   Comparison to USENET, 24
   Definition, 69-70, 236
   Digests, 70
   Directory of, 79-84
   Etiquette, 72, 224-225
   Moderated, 70
   Searching for, 70-71
   Subscribing to, 24, 71
   Unsubscribing, 24, 72
Management Advantage, 164
Management consultants, 163-165
Management Consulting Online, 164
Management Information Systems (MIS), 81
Management Recruiters International, 176, 177, 203
Manpower, 176
Manufacturing, 77
Mayo Online Career Center, 155
McAfee VirusScan, 228
Mediation, 165-167

Memory, 29-30
Mercer Inc., 131
MGTDEV-L, 83
Microsoft
  Exchange, 49
  Internet Explorer, 46, 48-49
  Internet News, 68-69
  Network, 25, 36-37
.mil, 23, 55, 90
MIME, *see* Multipurpose Internet Mail Extensions
Mirror site, 236
MIS, *see* Management Information Systems
Misc, 67
Misc.business.consulting, 79
Misc.business.records-management, 79
Misc.industry.quality, 79
Misc.jobs.contract, 79
Misc.jobs.misc, 79
Misc.legal.moderated, 79
Misc.taxes, 79
Modems, 30-31, 236
Modulator-demodulators, see Modems
Monster Board, 155, 176
Montara Connection, 134
Morgan Stanley lawsuit, 59
MSDS Online, 183
Multimedia Chatting, 73-74
Multi-purpose Internet Mail Extensions (MIME), 57, 236

National Association of Temporary and Staffing Services, 121, 203
National Association of Workforce Professionals, 121, 207
National Center for Employee Ownership, 140
National Council on Compensation Insurance, 183
National Crisis Prevention Institute, 217
National Employee Services and Recreation Association,

Index 257

121
National Institute of Occupational Safety and Health, 145, 183
National Institute of Pension Administrators, 121, 129
National Labor Relations Board, 159, 161, 167
National Organizational Development Network, 83
National Safety Council, 183
National Trauma Services, 217
Nationwide Advertising Service, 176
Navigator, see Netscape
NCSA Mosaic Access Page, 138-139, 144
.net, 23, 55, 90
Netcom, 42
Netiquette, 13, 60-61, 224-225, 236
Netscape, 26, 46-48, 56-59, 68, 73, 234
  Chat, 25, 73
  Communications, 58-59
  Communicator, 46, 57
  Mail, 56-57
  Navigator, 46-48
  Netsite, 226
  Newsreader, 68
Netsmart, 155
NetStart, 176-177, 194
Netsurfer Focus on Cryptography and Privacy, 227
Net Temps, 203
Network News Transfer Protocol (NNTP), 236
Networking, 19-20
New York State Department of Labor, 155
New Zealand, 83
News, 66
News Flashes, 155
Newsgroup post, 236
Newsgroup reader, 236
Newsgroups, 18, 21, 65-69, 77-79, 223, 236
  Categories, 66-68
  Definition of, 65, 236

Directory of, 77-79
FAQs, 11, 235
Searching, 21, 69, 103-109
Newsreader software, 68
Nijenrode Business Webserver for Human Resource Management & Organizational Behavior, 123
Nonprofit organizations, 79
North Carolina Human Resource Center, 146-147
NWAC-L, 83

Occupational Safety and Health Administration, 183
ODCNET-L, 83
ODNET, 83
Office Mates 5 from MRI, 177
Office of Economic Cooperation and Development, 199
Office of the American Workplace, 169
Offline, 237
Olsten Staffing Services, 177
Online, 237
Online Career Center, 142, 155, 164, 170-171, 177
Online Journal of Ethics, 187
Online Services, 14-16, 19, 32-39, 41, 43, 237
   Choosing between, 38-39
   Definition, 237
   Differences between Internet Service Providers and, 15-16, 32-33, 41
.org, 23, 55, 90
Organizational change, 80
Organizational development, 81, 83
Outplacement, 170-171

Pacific Bell, 201-202
Packets, 57-58, 237
Partnership Group, 135
PAYHR-L, 83
Payroll, 83, 171-172
Payroll Legal Alert, 172

Index

Peer Resources Homepage, 169
Pegasus, 54
Penn State Executive Programs, 207
Pension and Benefits, 129
Pension Benefit Guaranty Corporation, 129
People Lease, 203-204
People Pros Inc, 213
People Tech, 159
Personnel & Development Network, 136-137, 147
Personnel Concepts, 169-170
Personnel Office, 164-165
Personnel Systems Associates, 165
Plain Old Telephone Service (POTS), 31, 237
Plainfield, 148
Planning Your Future, 155-156
Point-to-Point Protocol (PPP), 41, 45-46, 245
Pornography, 229
Postmaster, 222
POTS, see Plain Old Telephone Service
PPP, see Point-to-Point Protocol
Presenting Solutions Inc., 195, 208
Pretty Good Privacy, 226
Prevention Online, 114
PRI Associates, 115, 195
PRIR-L, 83
Privacy, 233-235
Process Therapy Institute, 148
Prodigy, 5, 25, 37-38
Protocols, Internet, 5, 44-46, 95-96, 234, 234, 235, 236, 237
PSG International, 208
Psychology Associates, 208
Purdue Online Writing Laboratory Resume Workshop, 156

Qualcomm, 56-57
Quality, 78, 79, 172

Quality Media Resources, 60
Questar Corp., 195
Quoting, 72, 237

Racism
  Lawsuits, 59-60
Rec, 66
Records management, 79
Recruiters Online Network, 156, 177
Recruitment, 173-179
Recruitment and Training Administration, 177-178
Reinhart, Boenner, Van Deuren, Nomis & Rieselbach, 129-130
Relocation, 179-180
Relocation Journal, 179-180
Relocation Resources, 180
Restrac Inc., 178
Resumix, 156, 195
Retirement Plans for the Self-Employed, 129
Rio Communications, 187
Robert Rosell, 60
Rocky Mountain Employee Benefits Bulletin, 129-130
Ross Systems InfoCentral, 195
Router, 237
R.R. Donnelley & Sons lawsuit, 59
Runzheimer International, 180

S-HTTP, *see* Secured Hypertext Transport Protocol
Safe Hex for the Nineties, 228
Safety, 180-184
Safety Pays, 184
Salary Calculator, 180
Salary Guides, 134-135
Salary Information/Salary Survey Sites, 135, 180, 200
Salary Survey Sites, 135, 180, 200
Sales Leads USA, 132, 156
Saludos Web, 140

SAP America, 195
SAS Institute, 200
Sci, 66-67
Search engines, 102-109, 237
Search United States Government Documents, 161
Secure Newsgroups, 226
Secured Hypertext Transport Protocol, 226
Secured Sockets Layer (SSL), 234
Security, 49, 184-185, 225-227
Selection, 185-187
SER Jobs for Progress National, 115, 140, 144, 156
Serial Line Interface Protocol (SLIP), 41, 44-46, 237
Server, *see* File server
Sex Discrimination, 115
Sexual abuse, 78
Sexual harrassment, 59-60, 187-188
  Lawsuits, 59-60
Shareware, 237
Shouting, 60, 225, 237
Sierra Systems Consultants, 195-196
SIFT, *see* Stanford Information Filtering Tool
Simply Better, 178
Situation Management Systems Inc., 208
Small Business Administration, 170
Small Business Law Center, 162
Smoking, 78, 188
Snail mail, 238
Soc, 67
Social conduct, 224-225
Social Security Administration, 130
Society for Human Resource Management, 121-122, 135, 142-143
Soc.org.nonprofit, 79
Software, 136, 174, 178, 185, 188-198, 200, 204, 206-211
Software Plus, 196
Software Technology Corp., 178, 196

Sorehand, 84
Spectrum Human Resource Systems Corp., 197
Spiders, 104
SPRY, 54
SPSS, 200
Stanford Information Filtering Tool (SIFT), 69
StarGarden Quality Human Resources and Payroll Software, 197
State of Kentucky, 162
State of Wisconsin, 130
Statistics, 198-200
Statistics Canada, 200
STAT-USA, 200
Stay Out, 217-218
Steinberg Consultants Inc., 198
Strategic Communications Online, 143
Strategic Management Group, Inc., 197
SunGard Employee Benefit Systems, 130

Talk, 67
Target Vision, 197
Taxes, 79, 200-201
TCP/IP, see Transmission Control Protocol/Internet Protocol
Technical courtesy, 224-225
Technical support, 40
Technology, 82, 188-198, 201-202
Technology and employment, 82
Technology, HR & Communication Home Page, 143, 202
Techweb, 170, 178-179
TECo Enterprises Inc., 197
Telecommuting, 201-202
Telephone lines, 31-32, 235, 237
    Integrated Services Digital Network (ISDN), 31-32, 235
    Plain old telephone service (POTS), 31, 237
TELNET, 95-96
Temporary staffing, 202-204
TESLSB-L, 84

Thomas, 161
Thomas Register, 132
3 Ring Information Systems, 143
Time+Plus, 172, 197
TimeVision Inc., 197
Towers Perrin Online, 130-131
Training and development, 71, 84, 135-137, 204-211, 213
Training and Development List (TRDEV-L), 71, 84, 137, 210
Training and Development Resource Center, 137, 208, 213
Training and Seminar Locator, 208-209
Training Consortium, 209
Training Forum, 209
Training Net, 210
Training Source, 188, 210
Training Supersite, 210
Training Technology Resource Center, 210
Transmission Control Protocol/Internet Protocol (TCP/IP), 5, 41, 43, 238
Travis, 130
TRDEV-L, *see* Training and Development List
Typing injuries, 84

.Uk, 23
Ultimate Software Group, 198
Union-D, 84
Union Resource Network, 213
Unions, *see* Labor unions
Unite, 84
Universal Resource Locator, 22-23, 89-90, 238
University of Alberta, 149
University of California/Berkeley, 149, 188
University of Maryland Diversity Database, 140
University of Minnesota, 96
Unix-to-Unix Decode (uudecode), 58

Unix-to-Unix Encode (uuencode), 58, 238
Up-to-Date Library, 170
Upload, 238
URL, see Universal Resource Locator
.Us, 23
US Agency for Toxic Substances and Disease Registry, 180
US Code of Federal Regulations, 162-163
US Companies that are Doing Right, 159
US Department of Agriculture, 149
US Department of Energy, 184
US Department of Health and Human Services, 149-150
US Department of Justice, 137, 162
US Department of Labor, 125-126, 133-134, 144, 156, 183, 216
  Women's Bureau, 144, 216
US Government Printing Office, 161
US Group— Intersourcing Online, 179
US Health Care Financing Administration, 148
US House of Representatives Internet Law Library, 162-163
US Human Resources, 147
US Immigration for Canadian Businesses and Professionals, 163
US Internal Revenue Service, 201
US Library of Congress, 161
US Occupational Safety and Health Administration, 183
US Recruitment and Training Administration, 177
USENET, see Users Network
User name, 238
Users Network (USENET), 18, 21, 65-69, 103-109, 223, 238
  Definition, 18, 65, 238
  Organization of, 66-68
  Searching, 21, 69, 103-109
Usertech, 210
Uudecode, see Unix-to-Unix Decode

Uuencode, *see* Unix-to-Unix Encode
UVA's Video Display Ergonomics Page, 145

Veronica, *see* Very Easy Rodent-Oriented Net-wide Index to Computerized Archives (Veronica), 22
Very Easy Rodent-Oriented Net-wide Index to Computerized Archives (Veronica), 22, 98-99, 238
Video Display Ergonomics Page, 145
VideoFax Systems, 198
Videolearning Systems, 211
Violence at Work, 218
Virtual Job Fair, 179
Virtual Reality Modeling Language (VRML) reader, 47
Virus scanner software, 228
Viruses, 227-228
Voices vs. Violence, 218
VRML reader, *see* Virtual Reality Modeling Language reader

WAIS, *see* Wide Area Information Server
Wallis Co., 190
Watson Wyatt Insider, 130-131
Watson Wyatt Worldwide, 165
Web browsers, 46-50, 239
Web Crawler, 107-108
Web indexes, 211-215
Web pages, 88, 90-91, 228-229, 239
　Creating, 228-229
　Definition, 90, 238
Web sites, 19, 91, 113-218, 222, 239
　Creating, 228-229
　Definition, 91, 238
　Directory, 113-218
Webmaster, 222
Welltech Worksite Health Promotion Program, 150
Westech Career Expo, 156-157
Wharton School of the University of Pennsylvania, 131

What Color is Your Parachute? Job Hunting Online, 157
When You Have to Let Someone Go, 163
White House, 163
Wide Area Information Server, 100-101, 239
William M. Mercer Inc., 131
William Steinberg Consultants Inc., 198
WINGS, 157
Winning Associates, 165
Wisconsin, State of, 130
WISSAGO, 123
Women Against Sexual Harassment, 188, 216
Women's Bureau, 144, 216
Women's issues, 78, 115, 144, 188, 215-216
Women's Web, 216
Work Wise—Desktop and Intranet Solutions, 198
Workflow and Reengineering International Association, 122
Workforce Online, 170, 214
Workindex, 214
Worknet Job Search, 157
Workplace violence, 216-218
Workplace Violence Prevention Programs, 218
Workplace Violence Quiz, 218
World Health Organization, 150
World Wide Web, 19, 20, 87-91, 113-218, 239
   Definition of, 19, 88, 239
   Directory, 113-218
   How to find information on, 20
World Wide Web Consortium, 23
World Wide Web Yellow Pages, 132
WorldsChat, 73-74
Wyatt Insider, 131
Wyatt Worldwide, 165

Xalta Interactive, 198

Yahoo, 20, 108-109, 214-215
You First Health Risk Assessment, 150

MORAN ASSOCIATES

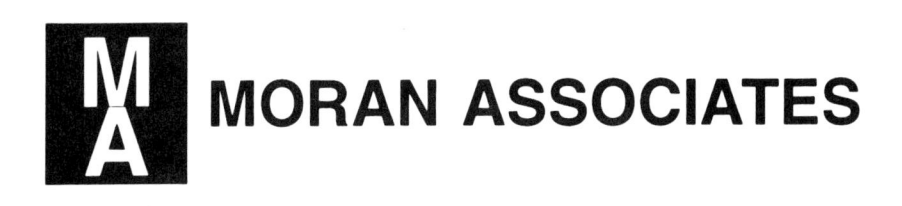

My Favorite Internet Resources

Internet Address	Notes

MORAN ASSOCIATES

Add or Update an HR Resource

Have you found a new human resources Web site or newsgroup? Maybe you have set up one of your own. Let us know so that we can be sure to include these new resources in future editions of this book.

Resource Name

_____

Description of Resource and Background

_____

_____

Resource Location

_____

Contact Information

Sponsor: _____

Sponsor's Address: _____

Telephone/Fax: _____

Contact Name: _____

Contact E-Mail: _____

Fax this form to MORAN ASSOCIATES at 904-278-5494
or mail it to:
     Moran Associates
     1600 Brighton Bluff Court
     Orange Park, FL 32073

MORAN ASSOCIATES

More Books and Software From MORAN ASSOCIATES...

THE OSHA ANSWER BOOK, 3rd Edition

This new edition includes answers to key questions on: OSHA standards, recordkeeping and reporting requirements? Every OSHA requirement is covered in this book. This book also contains the latest information on how to get safety and health information from the Internet. This is the only book your office will ever need to ensure compliance, reduce injuries and control workers compensation costs.
Softcover, 320 pages, 1994, ISBN: 0-9632296-7-2 **$49**

THE OSHA 500

A user-friendly index and compliance guide to more than 500 of the most cited OSHA standards. This book contains a 35-page alphabetical index that covers all recordkeeping regulations, all employee training requirements and all standards that require employers to adopt written compliance programs.
Three-ring Binder, 315 pages, 1991, ISBN: 0-9632296-9-9 **$99.95**

OSHAMETIC

OSHAMETIC is a Windows™ software program that lists all mandatory employee training regulations that apply to your business. OSHAMETIC contains all General Industry (1910) training regulations in one convenient easy-to-use program. It can help you exactly which OSHA regulations require you to provide training to your employees.
Software program for Windows™, 1995 **$99.95**

1600 Brighton Bluff Court, Orange Park, FL 32073
Phone: 1-800-597-2040 • Fax: 904-278-5494